ID Project Management

Tools and Techniques for Instructional Designers and Developers

Michael Greer
I. D. Network

Educational Technology Publications
Englewood Cliffs, New Jersey 07632

Library of Congress Cataloging-in-Publication Data

Greer, Michael.
    ID project management : tools and techniques for instructional
designers and developers / Michael Greer.
       p. cm.
    Includes bibliographical references and index.
    ISBN 0-87778-237-7
    1. Instructional systems--Design.   I. Title.
    LB1028.38.G74   1992   91-24618
    371.3′078—dc20   CIP

Printed in the United States of America.

Library of Congress Catalog Card Number:
91-24618.

International Standard Book Number:
0-87778-237-7.

First Printing: January 1992.

Dedication

For Bonnie, who's always there with love and support while challenging me to be my best.

Acknowledgments

Management doesn't happen in a vacuum; nor can a set of project management tools and techniques like those presented here spring full blown from the mind of one individual. On the contrary, this book represents a set of discoveries that has resulted from my exposure over the years to many talented people who have struggled to create effective instructional materials. Whether we were developing a mini-course in a public secondary school, a university self-study program, or new product training for a major high-tech company, the problems to be overcome by the design team remained largely the same. Subject Matter Experts had to be found and nurtured, money had to be obtained and wisely husbanded, the development schedule had to be maintained, and the sponsor and design team had to be kept reasonably happy. By working side-by-side with dedicated people who have met these challenges, I have been able to discern the patterns of what works and what doesn't work in ID project management. Because this book is largely a synthesis of these practices, it is only fitting that I acknowledge some of their more important origins.

In the early 1970s George Caras and Charles Cole established Tratec, a Los Angeles instructional development consulting firm that counted among its clients IBM, AT&T, Xerox, and many other major corporations. Over the years, some of the best and brightest instructional technologists in the country worked at Tratec as employees and as contractors. Some eventually left to start their own competitive consulting firms, many of which thrive today. As a designer and later a manager at this firm, I was introduced to tools and techniques that were designed to attain quality results, on time, and within the assigned budget. These tools and techniques worked. Tratec had a reputation for achieving excellent results. Many of the tools and techniques presented in this book can be traced to those pioneered at Tratec. While it would be impractical to list here by name the hundreds of professionals who, over the years, contributed to the evolution of Tratec's techniques, it is necessary to acknowledge the important role played by this organization in shaping the ideas presented in this book.

This book also owes much to Xerox Corporation's Marketing Education group and, in particular, to one of its former leaders, Dr. Anne Bloomer. In the mid-1980s Anne asked me to work with her to conduct an analysis of the ID project management practices of her organization and to recommend ways in which these practices could be improved. One result of this analysis was a five-day course for new ID project managers. This course contains many tools and techniques that I was able to make generic and use in later articles, workshops, and this book. Anne challenged me to refine my thinking about ID project management while, at the same time, serving as an internal change agent to assure adoption of the processes within her organization. Her skills and insights left their mark on many of the tools and techniques presented here.

I must also acknowledge the support of Dr. Sivasailam Thiagarajan, known simply as "Thiagi" to many in our field. As the editor of *Performance & Instruction,* the official journal of the National Society for Performance & Instruction (NSPI), he provided the encouragement needed to keep me writing the series of 10 articles about ID project management that eventually led to this book.

My thanks also to Dr. James Cole, former head of the College of Communication and Computer Information Sciences at Clarion University of Pennsylvania, where I obtained my graduate degree. In Dr. Cole's management class, I learned that without effective management, instructional technology might remain a mere wish in the hearts of few educators.

I must also acknowledge the support and encouragement of my editor, Lawrence Lipsitz, who helped me through the process of writing this book. He both challenged and encouraged me, while putting up with my occasional grumpiness.

Finally, I want to thank my wife and business partner, Bonnie. As financial manager for our company, she gave her personal attention to the worksheets that help estimate project scope, making several important improvements. More importantly, as my wife, she was patient and supportive when the hours budgeted for my writing extended into days.

Table of Contents

List of Tools and Techniques

Figures and Tables

Preface

Our Goals

In creating this book, we had three goals in mind:

- To define a specific, yet generic instructional development (ID) project management model.

- To describe specific actions to be taken by the ID project manager within the context of this management model.

- To provide specific tools and techniques that ID project managers may employ quickly so as to help their development teams create high-quality materials, on time, within budget.

Notice that the word "specific" appears in each of the goals. This book focuses **specifically** on the effective management of instructional development projects.

What This Book Is Not About!

This book is **not** about:

- General, all-purpose project management.

  We focus entirely on ID projects.

- General staff management.

  We focus on managing specific members of an instructional development team.

- Management of an instructional development department or instructional facility.

  We focus on linear ID projects that have clear beginning and end points. Such development projects may be followed by projects involving revision or further research, but they are primarily single, self-contained development events.

- Time management, effective interpersonal communication, proper hiring practices, proper firing practices, and so on.

  While all these are legitimate topics that might interest a manager, this book will stick entirely to the tools and techniques of managing instructional development.

Why ID Project Management?

Most people who manage ID projects have had either formal or informal exposure to the field of instructional development. As these people soon learn, there are all sorts of models and tools available to instructional developers. Indeed, the professional activities of the instructional developer have had the benefit of years of definition and refinement.

But the job of the ID project manager is not nearly so well defined. Like any manager, the ID project manager must complete projects within limited budgets and limited schedules. Yet good instructional development principles often collide with these "bottom-line" constraints. ID project managers must therefore walk a tightrope, suspended between their own ID conscience and their management's requirements for fast, cost-effective training.

In the face of these pressures and constraints, it is difficult to assure that effective instruction is created. The project manager must be able to perform exactly the right management interventions at exactly the right time.

By providing managers with a conceptual framework (i.e., a model) and the tools and techniques to make interventions within this framework, this book will help them quickly determine the proper course of action at any point in the development process.

Many who manage ID projects do not consider themselves professional managers. They are educators, instructional developers, or subject matter experts (SMEs). It is safe to say that most of these practitioners would not recognize instructional development project management as a unique profession. This book helps to define the profession of instructional development project management and provides detailed descriptions of plans and interventions that ID project managers must make.

Is This Book for You?

Our **primary audience** for this book consists of *people who manage ID projects*. These people typically have one or more projects under way in which they must research, develop, test, and produce courseware such as instructor manuals, videotapes, student materials, computer-based training, and so on. Their primary responsibility is to assure that the instructional developers and media professionals who are working on the project complete all their assignments on time, within budget, and to an acceptable quality level.

In business or industry, these people may be called *project manager*, *program manager*, or some other title which indicates their management responsibilities. Frequently, however, these people are members of a training staff who are assigned the job of managing a team of developers on an ad-hoc basis, in addition to their ongoing staff activities. They may use internal developers, hire contract or vendor developers, or perform some of the development chores themselves. Sometimes these people have had formal training in ID, while other times they have been successful subject matter experts or practitioners "brought in to training" from a particular field position. Seldom, however, is their role of ID project manager regarded as a unique discipline.

In academic settings, the primary audience for this book is even less likely to be called project manager. Typically, they are people associated with Learning Resource Centers, government-funded instructional development projects, schools of education, and so on. Like their business counterparts, they are often subject matter experts (professors) or general program coordinators managing an instructional development project on an ad-hoc basis. Also, like their business counterparts, they may use internal developers, hire contract or vendor developers, and perform some of the development chores themselves. In many cases they work without benefit of formal training in instructional development.

Besides this primary audience, **others who might benefit from this book** include:

Managers of organizations that employ instructional developers and ID project managers. These include Training Department managers, Human Resource Development managers, Documentation Department managers, Marketing and Public Relations Department managers, Curriculum Development Coordinators, and so on.

Instructional designers and developers who often must work without tight management guidelines or recognition of their management role in order to coordinate the efforts of many professionals. (All instructional developers must interact with so many different people during the project that they need to know as much as possible about project management.)

Others (often subject matter experts) without training department or ID titles who must figure out how to organize a project to develop instructional materials at the same time they are performing their other work chores.

In short, if you directly or indirectly try to make instructional development projects happen, you are likely to benefit from this book.

Chapter 1

An Overview of ID Project Management

This chapter presents an overview of the generic ID project management model and defines the role of the ID project manager during each step of the model. Before we tackle the model, however, we need to distinguish ID projects from ongoing ID programs.

A Distinction: ID Projects vs. Ongoing ID Programs

An **ID project** is typically a linear series of development events that culminates in a finished instructional product. For example, in a typical ID project, a needs analysis leads to a set of instructional objectives, which leads to a course design, which eventually results in a completed set of instructional materials. An **ongoing ID program**, on the other hand, is often non-linear and iterative. For example, such a program might consist of a series of evaluations of learner skills over several years' time, resulting in the specification and development of the appropriate instructional materials to meet learner deficiencies. In time, the implementation of these materials may be monitored and reevaluated, leading to the specification of still more development activities. Unlike the more focused ID project, the scope of an ongoing ID program may be extremely broad, such as that required to upgrade an entire curriculum.

Another distinction between ID projects and ongoing ID programs is method of funding. ID projects are typically funded on a per project basis; ongoing ID programs are usually funded based on a broad period of time, such as a fiscal year. For example, there may be $50,000 set aside for an ID project to develop a specific, two-day technical skills training course within a specific time frame. When the money is gone, the investors expect to have a set of completed courseware. On the other hand, in a typical ongoing ID program, the same $50,000 may be set aside yearly for ongoing evaluation, development, and implementation activities. When the money is gone from the year's ID program budget, the investors expect to see some tangible courseware, but they also would likely expect evaluation reports showing student improvement and analysis documents that make recommendations about further development or implementation requirements.

Table 1-1 summarizes the distinctions between ID projects and ID programs.

ID Projects	ID Programs
Linear series of events	Non-linear, iterative events
Limited in scope	Broad in scope
Funding by project	Funding by time
Culminate in specific finished products	Result in ongoing activities and products

Table 1-1: ID Projects vs. Ongoing ID Programs

The focus of this book is the ID project. That is, we will examine what is required to manage a linear, finite development effort resulting in specific finished courseware. Because nearly every ongoing ID program contains one or more ID projects, the reader who is interested in the management of ongoing ID programs will likely benefit from the information contained in this book.

Figure 1-1: The Project Manager as Juggler

Manager or Juggler?

In the early '60s, when TV variety shows flourished, a strange little man would sometimes appear on Ed Sullivan's stage and fill it with plates rapidly spinning high atop long, slender poles. You may have seen him. He'd place a pole in a certain spot, then center a plate on top and get it spinning just so. Then he'd place another and another until the stage was filled with a forest of spinning plates on poles. He'd then scurry back and forth, finding plates that were slowing down and wiggling their poles until they began to spin rapidly again.

Like the plate spinner, as project manager you are not directly involved in all the actions while they are happening, but you do get each action started and you keep it going when it starts to slow down. And also like him, you must carefully plan all your moves.

In broad terms, then, my success as a project manager depends on these three activities:

Planning — conceiving of the overall project and arranging for all project events to happen

Stimulating Action — getting each individual event started at the scheduled time

Intervening — observing when things aren't going according to plan, then taking action to get things back on track

This book is designed to help you, the ID project manager, with these activities. We will include tools to help you plan project events, stimulate action, and intervene as needed.

Assumptions

We are assuming that before a project begins you have conducted the necessary front-end analyses to assure that you have a real training need. That is, we are assuming you are ready to begin instructional development.

In addition, we are assuming that you have some experience developing instructional materials and in using basic ID jargon. Finally, we are assuming that you will be using a typical project management model something like the one described on the following page.

A Typical ID Project Management Model

A typical Project Management Model might be divided into three major phases. These phases include ten steps, each consisting of several activities.

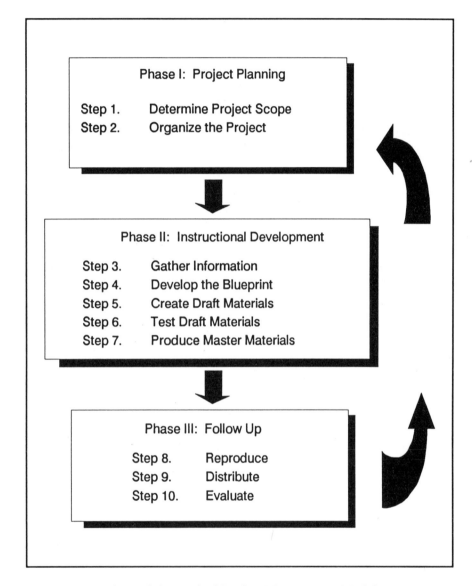

Figure 1-2: Typical Project Management Model

In the next few pages, we will provide an overview of each of these steps, including its specific purpose, activities that are typically performed in the step, and specific results or outputs of the step. In this way, you will get a "big picture" look at ID project management. Later, in the remaining chapters, we will examine all the steps in much greater detail, providing tools and techniques to help you manage the whole process.

Phase I: Project Planning

Step 1. Determine Project Scope

Purpose: When "selling" the project to internal or external sponsors, it is important for the project manager to make a preliminary guess at the project scope. This provides a "reality check," allowing everyone concerned to affirm his or her commitment to the project and its scope.

Activities: Make an early estimate of the amount of materials that must be created, the time and effort required to create them, and the resources required.

Results:

- ☐ Preliminary materials specifications
- ☐ A project schedule and/or time estimate
- ☐ A budget and/or cost estimate

Step 2. Organize the Project

Purpose: It is likely that substantial time will pass between the time the project scope is determined (Step 1) and the time that the project is authorized to begin. Therefore, the actual management of a project begins with *Step 2, Organize the Project*. This step requires the manager to confirm that the assumptions made about project scope are still valid. In addition, it requires that detailed plans be developed, thus helping to lay the groundwork for a successful project.

Activities: Confirm earlier assumptions about preliminary materials specifications, time, and costs. Confirm the project team members, set up the Project Diary, and organize the Kickoff meeting.

Results:

- ☐ A revised or confirmed set of materials specifications, schedule, and budget
- ☐ List of project team members
- ☐ Project Diary containing important project data
- ☐ A well-organized Kickoff meeting

Phase II: Instructional Development

Step 3. Gather Information

Purpose: Thorough information gathering assures that the right skills and concepts are provided by the training and that training dollars are invested wisely.

Activities: First, determine what kind of information is needed to support instructional development. Then, through observations, interviews, and review of documentation, gather that information in an effective manner. Formal task, job, or content analyses are often conducted.

Results:

Detailed information is gathered concerning:

- ☐ The target audience of the training
- ☐ The trainees' relevant work environment
- ☐ The specific tasks which must be learned
- ☐ Technical details about the course content

Step 4. Develop the Blueprint

Purpose: The Blueprint (design specifications) allows all relevant reviewers to look at course content and strategy at a point before a lot of energy is expended in writing text and transitions, formatting job aids, creating graphics or case studies, or writing scripts. This early review permits the design team to make substantive structural revisions while the course is still easily revisable.

Activities: Synthesize the information gathered in Step 3 and create a detailed description, or Blueprint, of the courseware to be developed. Share the Blueprint with reviewers and revise based upon their comments.

Results:

A Blueprint document that includes these parts:

☐ A "big picture" description of the instructional materials and course flow

☐ Specific performance objectives

☐ Specific instructional strategies to be employed to attain each objective

☐ A detailed outline of content to be included in support of each objective

☐ A summary of media and materials to be created to support each objective

☐ Formal approval of the Blueprint by the course sponsor

Step 5. Create Draft Materials

Purpose: Draft versions of all instructional materials should be created before expensive master materials are produced. These materials will then be reviewed, revised, tested, and finalized before production begins.

Activities: Create drafts of workbooks, job aids, lesson plans, media scripts, CAI screens, and any other materials. Review these with key subject matter experts and other members of the design team, then revise as needed.

Results:

☐ Preliminary and revised drafts of all materials

☐ Formal approval of drafts by the course sponsor

Step 6. Test Draft Materials

Purpose: A test run of the course is essential to make sure that the materials work as they were designed to work.

Activities: Assemble representative members of the target audience and test the draft materials while observing their performance. After the test, debrief trainees and observers and specify revisions. Review test results and revision specifications with the course sponsor.

Results:

☐ A test run of all courseware

☐ Detailed revision specifications, approved by the course sponsor

Step 7. Produce Master Materials

Purpose: The purpose of this step is to create professional quality masters of all course materials.

Activities: Produce final masters of print, audio, video, CAI, and any other materials.

Results:

☐ High-quality master materials that may be used to create correspondingly high-quality reproductions

☐ Formal approval of these masters by the course sponsor

Phase III: Follow Up

Step 8. Reproduce

Purpose: Make copies of all materials prior to distribution to trainees and instructors.

Activities: Reproduce all course materials in specified volumes.

Results:

☐ High-quality copies of all course materials, as defined by the design specifications

Step 9. Distribute

Purpose: The purpose of this step is to make sure that all materials are properly stored and/or disseminated.

Activities: Distribute copies of materials to the appropriate locations for storage and/or dissemination to trainees and instructors.

Results:

☐ Copies of materials, properly stored and distributed in a timely manner

Step 10. Evaluate

Purpose: The main purpose of evaluation is to determine the long-term effectiveness of the instructional materials that were created. A secondary purpose is to confirm that the assumptions made about effective instructional design strategies continue to remain valid.

Activities: After trainees complete the course, conduct follow-up analyses of their ability to perform skills on the job. Develop recommended revisions based on these analyses.

Results:

☐ Reports of trainee skill level after completing the training recommendations for revisions, if appropriate

☐ Recommendations for improving the instructional development process

The Job of the Project Manager

The project manager's job is to see to it that the preceding events all happen on time, within budget, and to an acceptable level of quality. The project manager does not directly perform instructional development tasks. Rather, he or she plans each step, stimulates action on the part of members of the design team, and then makes necessary interventions throughout the project. (Remember the plate spinner?)

As an overview, this section briefly identifies how the project manager is involved in each step of the model. Subsequent chapters will delve deeper into each step and suggest specific project manager activities.

Phase I: Project Planning

Step 1. Determine Project Scope

Project Manager's Job:

☐ Create (or directly supervise the creation of) the materials specifications, the project schedule or time estimate, and the project budget or cost estimate.

☐ Present these to sponsors for approval.

Step 2. Organize the Project

Project Manager's Job:

☐ Confirm and revise (if needed) materials specifications, the project schedule or time estimate, and the project budget or cost estimate.

☐ Hire or acquire project team members, set up the Project Diary, and organize/run the Kickoff meeting.

Phase II: Instructional Development

Step 3. Gather Information

Project Manager's Job:

☐ Review the plans of the designers to gather information and conduct analyses.

☐ Trouble-shoot to make sure subject matter experts (SMEs) and sponsor take necessary steps to help designers get information and documentation as quickly as possible.

☐ Attend critical or "high risk" information gathering sessions.

☐ Review the designers' findings to make sure they are comprehensive and accurate.

Step 4. Develop the Blueprint

Project Manager's Job:

☐ Establish a climate of creative problem-solving for the design team.

☐ Establish or approve the format of the Blueprint before designers begin to write it.

☐ Evaluate and approve the Blueprint prior to release to other reviewers.

☐ Coordinate and attend review and/or feedback sessions.

☐ Obtain written approval of drafts from the sponsor.

Step 5. Create Draft Materials

Project Manager's Job:

☐ Establish or approve the format of drafts before designers begin to write them.

☐ Evaluate and approve the drafts prior to their release to other reviewers.

☐ Coordinate and attend review and feedback sessions.

☐ Obtain written approval of drafts from the sponsor.

Step 6. Test Draft Materials

Project Manager's Job:

☐ Obtain the appropriate facilities and equipment, an instructor (if necessary), and members of the target audience for testing.

☐ Plan the test, including observation and debriefing strategies.

☐ Coordinate the test and debriefings.

☐ Assure that designers synthesize revision recommendations and present them to the sponsor.

☐ Obtain the sponsor's approval.

Step 7. Produce Master Materials

Project Manager's Job:

☐ Assure that revisions specified after the test are incorporated into the drafts.

☐ Plan the creation of master materials based on course specifications.

☐ Coordinate efforts of production personnel and designers as needed.

☐ Assure that final review and revisions are completed.

☐ Obtain sponsor's approval.

Phase III: Follow Up

Step 8. Reproduce

Project Manager's Job:

☐ Assure that materials are reproduced according to specifications.

Step 9. Distribute

Project Manager's Job:

☐ Assure that reproduced materials are properly distributed and stored.

Step 10. Evaluate

Project Manager's Job:

☐ Initiate and manage the follow-up evaluation of the completed course after it has been implemented.

Conclusion

The job of the ID project manager can be confusing and, at times, overwhelming. On the other hand, if properly orchestrated, it can be a lot of fun, resulting in quality courseware with minimum pain.

In the rest of this book we will examine each of the ten steps of the Project Management Model in detail. In particular, we will focus on what project managers can do to plan, to stimulate action, and, when necessary, to intervene in order to remove obstacles and achieve the project goals. To make these chores easier, we will provide guidelines and checklists for you to use on the job.

When you complete the book you will be better prepared to perform this important job with the precision and enthusiasm of our plate spinner. At the very least, you should be better prepared to control the storm of activities that makes up the instructional development process.

Chapter 2

How to Determine Project Scope

So far, we have introduced a 10-step project management model, along with an overview of the job of the project manager during each of these steps. In this chapter we will take a detailed look at the tasks required to complete Step 1: Determine Project Scope.

The Big Picture

An ID project, like any project that consumes resources, must be approved by top managers of the organization (i.e., the sponsors) before it can proceed. In effect, the project manager must "sell" the project to the organization's decision makers. But before selling the project, the project manager must make a preliminary guess at the project scope. Questions like "Exactly what are we going to develop? How much will it cost? How long will it take? How many people will we need?" must be addressed. Answers to these questions provide a "reality check," allowing everyone concerned to affirm his or her commitment to the project. What starts out as a great idea for training may, after project scoping, turn out to cost more or take more time and effort than anyone imagined.

To determine the scope of the project, you must first estimate the amount of materials that must be created, then the time and effort required to create them, and, finally, the cost. Figure 2-1 illustrates this process.

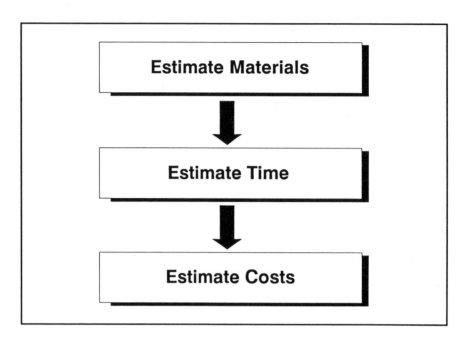

Figure 2-1: Determining Project Scope

Note the sequence of these activities. It's strictly linear. You can't estimate time required before you describe the materials you will be creating. And you can't estimate costs until you know the time (effort) required. Seem obvious? Maybe so. Yet you'd be surprised how often project budgets are built without detailed estimates of materials or time.

In any case, your goal as project manager is to come up with each of these estimates and present them to the sponsor (or buyer) of the project.

Estimating Required Materials

So the first task in determining project scope is to figure out what materials must be created. But how can you possibly estimate materials when you haven't written your performance objectives or gathered information about the content or the tasks to be learned?

Unfortunately, you seldom have a choice. You can't get approval to begin until you present your project schedule and budget to your sponsor. And you can't create a project schedule or budget until you make an estimate of effort — and that estimate is based on materials. So you're stuck with making an educated guess about required materials.

You can, however, take comfort from the fact that there are a few rules of thumb which instructional development managers have used for years to estimate the materials required. Using these rules of thumb, you can make a sensible estimate.

The key word at this point in the project is estimate. You are making a preliminary guess only. It need not be absolutely accurate. It must simply provide enough information for planning and negotiation.

Typical Materials Created

Below is a list of the typical kinds of materials that are created during the development cycle. You can use this list to help you think of all the materials that you might require.

- The Blueprint (or design specifications)
- Pages of workbook
- Pages of job aids and reference materials
- Scripts for audio-visual presentations
- Finished audio-visual presentation masters
- Pages of lesson plans
- Computer-assisted instruction flow charts, text frames, and branching instructions
- Professionally produced graphics
- Overhead transparencies
- Pages of general instructions for instructors or trainees describing facilities and equipment requirements, room set-up, and so on

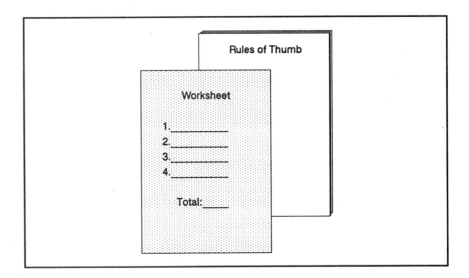

Figure 2-2: Tools for Estimating Materials

Tools for Estimating Materials

There are two tools required when you are making estimates of materials. A paper worksheet (or electronic spreadsheet) will help you keep a tally of the materials, while a set of guidelines (rules of thumb) will help you make your estimates.

Typical Worksheet: Estimating Materials Required

The sample worksheet on the next page could be used to estimate the required materials for a course consisting of some reading materials, media presentations, case studies, role plays, job aids, and other deliverables.

A close examination of this worksheet reveals that it is based on a lot of different rules of thumb. Let's look at some of these.

On the first line we can enter the number of hours we estimate people will spend reading our text materials. This is then multiplied by 20 pages to determine the total reading (text) materials required. The rule of thumb, therefore, is that people will be able to read about 20 pages per hour of our text materials.

The next part of the worksheet assumes we will guess the number of minutes of audio and video that must be created and multiply it by a factor to determine the length of the script that must be written. The rule of thumb used is that we will need to create 1 1/3 pages of script for every minute of audio and 2 pages of script for every minute of video. The rest of the worksheet uses similar rules of thumb to help provide a concrete summary of pages of instructional materials that must be created.

Note the bottom of the worksheet, under "Blueprint." This section assumes that you will be creating a Blueprint (set of design specifications) that will be either 1/2 or 1/3 the volume of the entire set of instructional materials. Let's say, for example, you have completed the top part of the worksheet and determined that you will be creating 150 pages of instructional materials. If you expect these materials to be complex or controversial, you might want to build a Blueprint that is very detailed so that you can get lots of feedback from your reviewers. In this case you would estimate your Blueprint to be 75 pages (150 divided by 2). If you expect the materials to be fairly straightforward, you may plan on a less detailed Blueprint of only 50 pages (150 divided by 3).

Worksheet: Estimating Materials Required

Reading Materials: _____ hrs. X 20 pages = _____

Audio script: 1 1/3 X _____ (# minutes) = _____

Video script: 2 X _____ (# minutes) = _____

Introduction and Summaries for Media:

    Audio: 1/2 X _____ (# of segments) = _____

    Video: 1/2 X _____ (# of segments) = _____

Instructor Orientation Notes (10 - 15 pages) = _____

Lesson Plan or Lecture Notes:

    15 X _____ (# of hours lecture) = _____

Overheads or Flip Charts:

    10 X _____ (# of hours lecture) = _____

Case Studies, Role Plays, Quizzes:

    Instructor Guidelines: _____

    Describe Situations: _____

    Describe Roles: _____

    Assign Tasks: _____

    Give Solution/Feedback: _____

    Step-by-step Instructions: _____

    Quiz Questions, Answers: _____

    Job Aids, Other Reference Materials: _____

    Miscellaneous Materials: _____

Total Pages of Instructional Materials: _____

Blueprint (choose one):

	TOTAL PAGES	
Blueprint, complex materials:	2	_____

or

	TOTAL PAGES	
Blueprint, straightforward materials:	3	_____

Typical Rules of Thumb: Estimating Materials Required

On the next page is a typical set of rules of thumb that you might use to estimate materials required.

CAUTION: The worksheet and rules of thumb presented here are only examples. They are based on assumptions that may or may not be useful in your organization. In order for you to make your own estimates of materials required you should set up a similar worksheet, either on paper or on an electronic spreadsheet. You will also need to assemble some rules of thumb that you can trust. These are available from a number of industry sources. The best rules of thumb, however, are ones that are specific to your organization. These can be obtained by reviewing completed projects and by talking to your fellow project managers.

By the way, one of our favorite ways of estimating materials does not require any rules of thumb. You simply look in your library for an existing course that seems to be similar to the course you intend to build. When you find one, you then count up the pages of materials, minutes of script, and other materials. You then compare this course to the one you intend to build and make your materials estimate.

Rules of Thumb: Estimating Materials Required

This reference aid will help you estimate specifically how many units of each type of material you will need to satisfy your course requirements.

Some Magical Numbers

Here are a few numbers used by some old hands in the training business to estimate the amount of materials required for courses:

Reading Materials

Rule: Up to 20 pages for each hour of trainee reading

Explanation: These include anything that trainees are asked to read (class handouts, text of workbooks, etc. Exercises and quizzes are not included.)

Audio and Video Scripts

Rule: About 1 1/3 pages of script for each minute of audio, 2 pages of script for each minute of video. Storyboards may take more pages per minute.

Explanation: If you intend to have your designers write their own scripts, use this rule of thumb. If your media contractors will be writing the scripts as part of a fixed price bid, then simply tell them how many minutes you will need.

Introductions and Summaries for Audio or Video Segments

Rule: About 1/2 page for each introduction or summary

Explanation: These "set-ups" or reviews may be required in trainee and/or instructor materials, especially when the productions are lengthy or complex. Explanations for overhead transparencies should not be considered here, but counted as part of the lesson plan (lecture) notes.

Instructor Orientation Materials

Rule: 10 or 15 pages for the average course

Explanation: This material describes general instructor skills required, facilities and set-up requirements, overall expectations regarding the "orchestration" of events, etc.

Lesson Plan (Lecture) Notes

Rule: About 15 pages for every hour of lesson plans

Explanation: Lecture notes are assumed to be outlined, bulleted lists of the points to be discussed by the instructor when teaching the course.

Overhead Transparencies or Flip Chart Visuals

Rule: About 10 per hour of lecture

Explanation: Be careful with this one! Complex materials can require substantially more visuals. Consider examining those used in a similar, existing course before deciding on a specific number.

Course Blueprint

(Estimate the Blueprint **after** all other estimates have been made.)

Rule: Complex materials - 1 page of Blueprint for every 2 pages of finished materials; Straightforward materials - 1 page of Blueprint for every 3 pages of finished materials.

Explanation: If your course materials will be complex or controversial, plan on building a thorough Blueprint so that reviewers will have lots of detail to react to. This will save time and money in the long run.

When you must create materials for which there are no rules of thumb available, the best thing to do is look to the past. Find a copy of a course similar to the one you must build and count how many pages of the various materials were built. Then you will simply have to take your best shot at an estimate.

Case Studies, Role Plays, and Quizzes

There are no reliable numbers available to help estimate case studies, role plays, and quizzes. These vary too greatly, depending upon course objectives and content. If you will be developing these kinds of materials, ask yourself the questions below.

Ask Yourself: How many pages will be required to completely describe the case study or role play **situation**? ... the **roles**? ... the required task or **assignment**? ... the "school **solution**?" ... special **instructor guidelines**?

How many pages of **reference materials** will you need to allow trainees to solve the problem?

How many pages of **step-by-step instructions** will you need to guide trainees through hands-on activities? (Think about each activity separately when estimating.)

How many tasks will require supporting **job aids**? What will these look like?

How often will trainees be given quizzes in the course and how many pages of **quiz questions and answers** will be created?

Case Study Example 1: Estimating Materials Required

Now let's examine how you might use this worksheet and the accompanying rules of thumb to estimate materials for a particular development effort. Here's the situation:

You have been talking to a sponsor about a one-day (6-hour) course. The course is based on content that is fairly straightforward. That is, everyone agrees on the main principles; the details are somewhat technical, but unarguable; and training objectives appear to be fairly clear-cut.

The course will be presented monthly at the corporate headquarters by full-time training people. They demand that courses be easy to administer, self-contained, and employ highly professional materials.

You are alone in your office, trying to develop your materials specifications. You've reviewed some existing courseware which ought to serve as a reasonably close approximation of the course, at least in terms of structure and layout.

You need to get on with creating your preliminary schedule and budget. But first, of course, you must complete your estimate of materials. You take a deep breath, swallow hard, and decide to go with **the following general design decisions:**

Two hours of the course will be self-paced instruction (mostly reading). In addition to the materials designed purely for reading, this part of the course will also include:

- 15 pages of step-by-step practice instructions

- 5 pages of performance aids for use on the job later

- A conceptual quiz that is 5 pages long

Four hours of the course will be instructor-led (primarily lecture-discussion, with a moderate number of overhead transparencies). This part of the course will require:

- 2 video tapes: one will be about 3 minutes long, the other will be about 15 minutes long

- 1 audio tape, 5 minutes long

- A 30-minute role play (one case situation, involving 4 different student roles)

The course designer will write the scripts for all media.
Given this situation, there are two questions to answer:
1. *How many pages of materials must be created?*
2. *How many pages of Blueprint must be created?*
Here's how your completed worksheet might look:

Solution to Case Study Example 1

Reading Materials: __2__ hrs. X 20 pages =   __40__

Audio script: 1 1/3 X __5__ (# minutes) =   __7__
                                                              (rounded)

Video script: 2 X __18__ (# minutes) =   __36__
Introduction and Summaries for Media:

    Audio: 1/2 X __1__ (# of segments) =   __1__
                                                              (rounded)

    Video: 1/2 X __4__ (# of segments) =   __2__

Instructor Orientation Notes (10 - 15 pages) =   __10__

Lesson Plan or Lecture Notes:

    15 X __4__ (# of hours lecture) =   __60__

Overheads or Flip Charts:

    10 X __4__ (# of hours lecture) =   __40__

Case Studies, Role Plays, Quizzes:

    Instructor Guidelines: __5__

    Describe Situations: __1__

    Describe Roles: __4__

    (1 page each X 4 roles)

    Assign Tasks: __4__

    (1 page each X 4 roles)

    Give Solution/Feedback: __4__

    (1 page each X 4 roles)

    Step-by-step Instructions: __15__

    (from self-paced materials)

    Quiz Questions, Answers: __10__

    (5 pages questions, 5 pages answers, from
    self-paced materials)

    Job Aids, Other Reference Materials: __5__

    Miscellaneous Materials: _____

Total Pages of Instructional Materials: __244__

Blueprint (choose one):

Blueprint, complex materials:	TOTAL PAGES 2	
		or
Blueprint, straightforward materials:	TOTAL PAGES 3	__81__

(Use this formula because materials are not controversial)

Estimating Time Required

The second major task in estimating project scope is to make a guess at how long it will take you to develop the materials. This can get a bit tricky, since there are essentially two types of time consumed during an instructional development project: consulting time and development time. As project manager you need to know how much of each you will be spending.

Consulting Time

Consulting time consists of the time spent in performing professional services, as opposed to creating tangible materials. Consulting time includes time spent when members of the design team:

- Determine project scope.

- Plan the project and hold meetings to discuss scope.

- Gather information, analyze the population, analyze the task, analyze content, and so on.

- Brainstorm and coordinate among members of the development team.

- Review (quality assure) materials before they are seen by the sponsor.

- Review and obtain feedback or approval from the sponsor.

- Set up, run, and observe pilot test sessions.

- Interact with production people to assure that the materials created meet specifications.

These activities usually account for 80% of the time spent by instructional designers and their managers during a typical development project. Because these activities are essential to creating high-quality, performance-based materials, it is important that they are planned for in the project schedule.

Development Time

Development time is time spent solely in creating instructional materials. Examples of development time include the time expended when designers:

- Write the Blueprint.

- Write the draft materials.

- Revise the draft materials for the test and for production.

While development time is essential to the creation of effective instructional materials, it usually accounts for only about 20% of the time spent in a typical project.

Novice project managers (and many course sponsors) often believe the development process to consist primarily of writing. This can lead to project schedules which have little or no consulting time allocated. As the pie chart below implies, the consulting activities must be as carefully planned as the development activities.

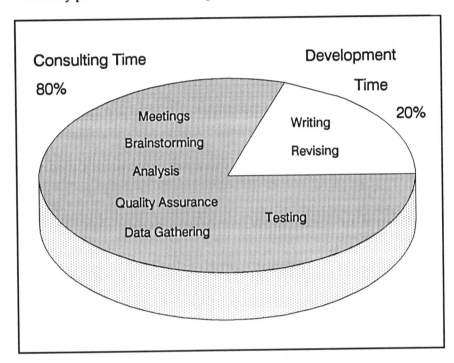

Figure 2-3: Consulting Time vs. Development Time

Tools for Estimating Time Required

The two basic tools for estimating time are the same as those required for estimating materials. You will need a worksheet (or electronic spreadsheet) and a set of guidelines (rules of thumb).

Typical Worksheet: Estimating Time Required

On the next page is a sample worksheet for estimating time. It is designed to help you capture two different types of information: days of labor required and calendar time required.

In the columns labeled "Mgr. Days" and "ID Days" you can fill in the number of days that you estimate will be spent by the project manager and the Instructional Designer or Developer. Later on, you can use this information to help determine labor costs and detailed calendars for the manager and ID.

In the column labeled "Schedule Duration" you can enter the number of days that a particular activity will take, regardless of how much time will be spent by the manager or ID. For example, a review of draft materials by subject matter experts may require 5 days of time in the schedule, yet no time will be spent by the manager or ID. By entering "5 days" in the Schedule Duration column, you will capture this time in your overall time estimate. Later, when you build a detailed calendar of project events, you will be able to include these 5 days of review.

Figure 4 illustrates how the first two columns of the worksheet capture information that you can use later to make job assignments and labor cost estimates, while the third column, "Schedule Duration," will help you build your specific project calendar.

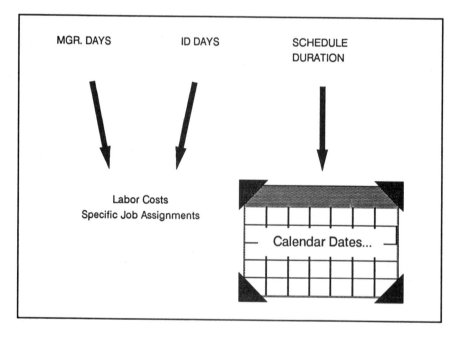

Figure 2-4: Uses for Information Captured

Worksheet: Estimating Project Time

STEP	MGR. DAYS	ID DAYS	SCHEDULE DURATION ~
1. Determine Project Scope			
Create preliminary project estimates:	_____	_____	
2. Organize the Project			
Confirm preliminary specifications:	_____	_____	_____
Hire or acquire project team members:	_____	_____	_____
Set up Project Diary; plan Kickoff:	_____	_____	_____
Conduct Kickoff meeting:	_____	_____	_____
Total Steps 1 & 2:	═══════════	═══════════	═══════════
3. Gather Information			
Plan information gathering strategy:	_____	_____	_____
Gather information:	_____	_____	_____
Total Step 3:	═══════════	═══════════	═══════════

~ Note: **"Schedule Duration"** is the number of consecutive work days required, regardless of time to be spent by ID or Manager. For example, during audio production, the ID may be required 2 days, the Manager required 1 day, while the Schedule Duration needed for the entire production may be 10 working days.

STEP	MGR. DAYS	ID DAYS	SCHEDULE DURATION

4. Develop the Blueprint

Get designer(s) started: _____ _____ _____

Write Blueprint: _____ _____ _____

Review Blueprint prior to review by SME/sponsor: _____ _____ _____

Sponsor review: _____ _____ _____

Meet with sponsor; feedback and approval: _____ _____ _____

Total Step 4: ========= ========= =========

5. Create Draft Materials

Get designer(s) started: _____ _____ _____

Write materials: _____ _____ _____

Review, discuss, revise prior to SME/sponsor review: _____ _____ _____

Sponsor review privately: _____ _____ _____

Meet with sponsor; feedback and approval: _____ _____ _____

Revise drafts after sponsor review: _____ _____ _____

Total Step 5: ========= ========= =========

6. Test Draft Materials

Make copies, plan test, set up test site, rehearse: _____ _____ _____

Run course: _____ _____ _____

Debrief with students, instructors, and observers: _____ _____ _____

Total Step 6: ========= ========= =========

7. Produce the Masters

STEP	MGR. DAYS	ID DAYS	SCHEDULE DURATION
Revise drafts based upon test results:	_____	_____	_____
Have materials copy edited and revised:	_____	_____	_____
Meet with production people, review specifications:	_____	_____	_____
Time needed to produce masters:	_____	_____	_____
Prepare for review of masters:	_____	_____	_____
Review finished master materials with sponsor:	_____	_____	_____
Review masters and specify revisions to producers:	_____	_____	_____
Have producers revise masters:	_____	_____	_____
Total Step 7:	_____	_____	_____

8. Reproduce

STEP	MGR. DAYS	ID DAYS	SCHEDULE DURATION
Plan reproduction:	_____	_____	_____
Meet with repro people and review repro specifications:	_____	_____	_____
Reproduce materials:	_____	_____	_____
Spot check samples:	_____	_____	_____
Total Step 8:	_____	_____	_____

STEP	MGR. DAYS	ID DAYS	SCHEDULE DURATION
9. Distribute			
Distribute materials:	═══════	═══════	═══════
10. Evaluate			
Plan evaluation strategy:	_____	_____	_____
Conduct evaluation:	_____	_____	_____
Write up results/make recommendations:	_____	_____	_____
Present results and recommendations:	_____	_____	_____
Total Step 10:	═══════	═══════	═══════

Summary Time Estimate

	MGR. DAYS	ID DAYS	SCHEDULE DURATION
Total Steps 1 & 2. Scope/Organize	_____	_____	_____
Total Step 3. Gather Information	_____	_____	_____
Total Step 4. Develop the Blueprint	_____	_____	_____
Total Step 5. Create Draft Materials	_____	_____	_____
Total Step 6. Test Draft Materials	_____	_____	_____
Total Step 7. Produce the Masters	_____	_____	_____
Total Step 8. Reproduce	_____	_____	_____
Total Step 9. Distribute	_____	_____	_____
Total Step 10. Evaluate	_____	_____	_____
GRAND TOTAL, ALL STEPS:	═══════	═══════	═══════

Some Rules of Thumb for Estimating Time

In order to fill in the preceding worksheet, you will need some rules of thumb for estimating time at each step of the project. Here are some generic guidelines.

CAUTION: If any of these guidelines don't seem to make sense in your environment, then ignore them and use your own. Always trust your own experience or your organization's history when selecting appropriate rules of thumb.

Typical Rules of Thumb for Estimating Time

Overview

Each stage of the development process involves the completion of specific activities. The amount of time required to complete these activities will depend on the complexity of the materials, the number of materials required, and the number of people who are on the design team.

To make your time estimate, review these rules of thumb then apply your best judgment.

Step 1. Determine Project Scope

This step is usually not included in the time estimate. However, if you want to recover the value of time spent, you should keep track of the days managers spend performing this activity for the project and fill it in on the worksheet. This will assure that the time is included in the cost estimate later.

Step 2. Organize the Project

This project planning stage typically takes anywhere from 10 to 20 working days, depending on the complexity of the project. The manager will be involved full time. ID time is optional, depending on how much the manager consults the ID. In any case, ID time will probably be no more than one-half the time spent by the manager. Some typical numbers include:

- Confirm and/or revise preliminary materials specifications, time estimates, and cost estimates: 3 days

- Hire or acquire project team members: 4 days (10 days, if using a vendor and soliciting bids, etc.)

- Set up Project Diary and plan Kickoff meeting: 2 days

- Conduct Kickoff meeting: 1 day

Step 3. Gather Information

Two activities consume time here:

- Plan information gathering strategy: 1 or 2 days

- Gather information: 5 to 10 days

Complex information, inaccessible SMEs, unstable content, and traveling to meet with widely distributed members of the target audience are examples of things that can increase the time needed. Plan accordingly.

(ID time: 100% of overall elapsed time. Manager [Mgr.] time : up to 75% of elapsed time.)

Step 4. Develop the Blueprint

This stage involves planning, writing, and review. Expect to spend the following time on these activities:

- Get the designer(s) started: 1/2 to 1 day (Both Mgr. and ID)

- Write the Blueprint: 1 day writing for every 10 pages of Blueprint. (For cut and dried material, you might consider 1 day for every 12 pages; more difficult content may require 1 day for every 6 to 8 pages. All writing time is spent by the ID only. Figures assume a quiet, uninterrupted writing place.)

- Review the Blueprint, then discuss and revise prior to review by sponsor and/or SMEs: 2 to 4 days (Both Mgr. and ID)

- Allow the sponsor to review the Blueprint in private: 2 to 5 days (This extends the schedule, but does not require ID or manager time.)

- Meet with the sponsor to obtain feedback and approval: 1 or 2 days (Both Mgr. and ID)

Step 5. Create Draft Materials

This stage also involves planning, writing, and review. Expect to spend the following:

- Get the designer(s) started: 1/2 to 1 day (Both Mgr. and ID)

- Write the materials: 1 day writing for every 10 pages of materials (For cut and dried material, you might consider 1 day for every 12 pages; more difficult content may require 1 day for every 6 to 8 pages. All writing time is spent by the ID only. Figures assume a quiet, uninterrupted writing place.)

- Review the materials, then discuss and revise prior to review by sponsor and/or SMEs: 2 to 4 days (Both Mgr. and ID)

- Allow the sponsor to review the materials in private: 3 to 5 days (This extends the schedule, but does not require ID or manager time.)

- Meet with the sponsor to obtain feedback and approval: 1 or 2 days (Both Mgr. and ID)

- Revise drafts after sponsor review: 2 to 10 days (depends on course complexity - ID only)

Step 6. Test Draft Materials

Include the following time:

- Make copies of materials, plan the test, set up the test site, and rehearse the instructor: 5 to 10 days (Mgr., 50%; ID, 100%)

- Run the course: [Assume actual number of days the course is designed to run.] (Mgr. & ID, 100%)

- Debrief with students, instructors, and observers: 1 or 2 days. (Mgr. & ID, 100%)

Step 7. Produce Master Materials

Include the following time:

- Revise drafts based upon test results: 3 to 7 days (ID, 100%; Mgr., 25%)

- Have the materials copy edited and revised: 1 to 3 days (ID, 50%)

- Meet with production people and review production specifications: 1 to 3 days (ID, 100%; Mgr., 50%)

- Schedule time needed for producing master materials (audio-visual and print are produced concurrently): 5 to 10 days (ID and/or Mgr. at video shoots, recording sessions, and editing sessions only — 5 to 7 days maximum.)

- Prepare for review of the masters: 1 or 2 days (ID, 100%; Mgr., 50%)

- Review the finished master materials with the sponsor: 1 or 2 days (ID, 100%; Mgr., optional, up to 100%)

- Review the masters and specify revisions to producers: 1 or 2 days (ID or Mgr., 100%)

- Have producers revise masters: 3 to 5 days (ID, 50%; Mgr., 25%)

Step 8. Reproduce

- Plan reproduction: .5 to 1 day   (ID or Mgr., 100%)

- Meet with reproduction people and review reproduction specifications: .5 to 1 day   (ID or Mgr., 100%)

- Reproduce materials: 15 to 20 working days (This extends the schedule, but only requires 1 or 2 days of ID or manager time.)

- Spot check samples of materials: .5 to 1 day   (ID or Mgr., 100%)

Step 9. Distribute

- Distribute materials: 1 day (by expensive, next-day air) to 2 weeks, depending on method of transport chosen and storage circumstances. (This extends the schedule, but only requires 1 day, at most, of ID or manager time.)

- Plan the evaluation strategy: Time required varies; could be a few days or a few weeks. (ID and Mgr. roles also vary from situation to situation.)

- Conduct the evaluation: Again, time required varies. This must be determined case by case.

- Write up the results of the evaluation and make recommendations: Time required varies.

- Present the results and recommendations and decide where to go from here: Time required varies.

Can You Really Save Time with More Designers on the Team?

If your course materials may be divided into self-contained parts, you might consider assigning additional designers for each additional part. For example, one designer might write the training for the technical people, another might write the customer training, and still another might write the training for the sales people. This could save you some time in gathering information (Step 3), developing the Blueprint (Step 4), creating draft materials (Step 5), and testing draft materials (Step 6).

The other development activities, including planning, analysis, reviews, and production/reproduction, will not show substantial time savings.

Warning: If you choose to add other designers, they should be hired early so they can participate in all stages from 3 (Gather Information) through 5 (Try Out the Materials and Revise). It will never save time to add a new designer at Step 5, Create Draft Materials. This person will need far too much coaching and will likely not create materials of the same quality as the designer who has helped mold the course from scratch.

Case Study Example 2: Estimating Time Required

Now let's examine how you might use this worksheet and the accompanying rules of thumb to estimate time needed for a particular development effort. In this example, we'll continue with the project from Case Study Example 1. Here's the situation:

Earlier you figured out how many materials were required for a one-day course. In this case study, you will try to figure out how much time is needed to create these materials.

So far, **you know this much:**

- You expect to use two different outside vendors; one as an instructional designer (who will also write A-V scripts) and one for audio-visual production. Both should have solid track records in their particular fields. At the moment, these vendors are not yet chosen.

- The ID will not be involved in any project activities until the Kickoff meeting.

- While the information to be gathered is fairly straightforward, the audience and the jobs they perform are somewhat cloudy. Therefore, you plan to spend time on a task analysis.

- Print production will be handled in-house, at your Print Center. They have promised a three-week turnaround on reproduced print materials.

- Your current course plan need not consider distribution or evaluation. In addition, you will not try to recover the time spent scoping the project.

Given this situation, there are three questions that must be answered:
  1. *How many working days will it take to complete this development effort?*
  2. *How many days of ID time are required?*
  3. *How many days of manager time are required?*

Here's how your completed worksheet might look:

Solution to Case Study Example 2

STEP	MGR. DAYS	ID DAYS	SCHEDULE DURATION ~
1. Determine Project Scope	*(Not applicable to this project)*		

2. Organize the Project

	MGR. DAYS	ID DAYS	SCHEDULE DURATION ~
Confirm preliminary specifications:	3	0	3
Hire or acquire project team members:	10	0	10

It will take extra time to prepare RFPs and choose the vendors. They will not officially start work on the project, however, until the Kickoff meeting.

	MGR. DAYS	ID DAYS	SCHEDULE DURATION ~
Set up Project Diary; plan Kickoff:	2	0	2
Conduct Kickoff meeting:	1	1	1
Total Steps 1 & 2:	16	1	16

3. Gather Information

	MGR. DAYS	ID DAYS	SCHEDULE DURATION ~
Plan information gathering strategy:	2	2	2

Planning the task analysis will take some thought. Better count on using these days to explore all possibilities.

	MGR. DAYS	ID DAYS	SCHEDULE DURATION ~
Gather information:	6	10	10

A thorough analysis will require the maximum of 10 days.

	MGR. DAYS	ID DAYS	SCHEDULE DURATION ~
Total Step 3:	8	12	12

4. Develop the Blueprint

	MGR. DAYS	ID DAYS	SCHEDULE DURATION ~
Get designer(s) started:	1	1	1

This first day ought to be spent brainstorming about possible design strategies and clarifying your requirements and format of the blueprint.

STEP	MGR. DAYS	ID DAYS	SCHEDULE DURATION
Write Blueprint:	0	7	7

The Blueprint will be 81 pages long. The designer is an experienced vendor and the materials are non-controversial and straightforward. Therefore plan on 12 pages per day to write the Blueprint. 81 divided by 12 = 6.75 or 7 days.

	MGR. DAYS	ID DAYS	SCHEDULE DURATION
Review Blueprint prior to review by SME/sponsor:	2	2	2

A well-planned Blueprint, written by an experienced designer, should require minimum review and revision prior to giving it to the sponsor. Two days should be plenty.

	MGR. DAYS	ID DAYS	SCHEDULE DURATION
Sponsor review:	0	0	2

Again, non-controversial material should require minimum review time.

	MGR. DAYS	ID DAYS	SCHEDULE DURATION
Meet with sponsor; feedback and approval:	1	1	1
Total Step 4:	4	11	13

5. Create Draft Materials

	MGR. DAYS	ID DAYS	SCHEDULE DURATION
Get designer(s) started:	1	1	1

Our experienced vendor designer should require little to get him or her started writing drafts. This time should be spent clarifying issues related to physical format of the drafts and, briefly, discussing how the design strategy from the Blueprint will be brought to life.

	MGR. DAYS	ID DAYS	SCHEDULE DURATION
Write materials:	0	20	20

Drafts will be 243 pages long. At 12 pages per day, that will be 20.25 or 20 days.

	MGR. DAYS	ID DAYS	SCHEDULE DURATION
Review, discuss, revise prior to SME/sponsor review:	3	3	3
Sponsor review privately:	0	0	3
Meet with sponsor; feedback and approval:	1	1	1
Revise drafts after sponsor review:	0	2	2

We are betting that the materials will emerge relatively untouched by the sponsor, requiring only minor revisions.

STEP	MGR. DAYS	ID DAYS	SCHEDULE DURATION
Total Step 5:	5	27	30

6. Test Draft Materials

Make copies, plan test, set up test site, rehearse:	4	7	7

While the course content is likely to be under control, the orchestration will be tricky (part self-paced and part instructor-led). Allow a moderate amount of time here.

Run course:	1	1	1
Debrief with students, instructors, and observers:	1	1	1
Total Step 6:	6	9	9

7. Produce the Masters

Revise drafts based upon test results:	1	5	5
Have materials copy edited and revised:	0	1	2
Meet with production people, review specifications:	1	2	2

We'll spend a day with the print producers and a day with the audio-visual people.

Time needed to produce masters:	3	7	10

Plan on the ID spending about 4 days at video shooting, a day at audio recording, and 2 days at editing sessions.

Prepare for review of masters:	1	2	2

There will be several different forms of masters to organize for client review. This will take at least 2 days.

Review finished master materials with sponsor:	1	1	1
Review masters and specify revisions to producers:	0	1	1
Have producers revise masters:	1	2	4
Total Step 7:	8	21	27

STEP	MGR. DAYS	ID DAYS	SCHEDULE DURATION

8. Reproduce

	MGR. DAYS	ID DAYS	SCHEDULE DURATION
Plan reproduction:	0	1	1

Several different media formats mean there will be lots of questions about reproduction and packaging. This will take some planning before meeting with repro people.

	MGR. DAYS	ID DAYS	SCHEDULE DURATION
Meet with repro people and review repro specifications:	0	1	1
Reproduce materials:	0	1	15

Our Print Center promised a three-week (15 working days) turnaround. Print always takes longer to reproduce than electronic media, so the maximum time here will be 15 days.

	MGR. DAYS	ID DAYS	SCHEDULE DURATION
Spot check samples:	0	1	(during)

It will probably take a few hours here and there (totaling no more than a day) to spot check samples of materials that are being reproduced. Since this will occur during the 15 day repro cycle, it will have no impact on schedule duration.

	MGR. DAYS	ID DAYS	SCHEDULE DURATION
Total Step 8:	0	4	17

9. Distribute & 10. Evaluate   *(Not applicable to this project.)*

Summary Time Estimate

	MGR. DAYS	ID DAYS	SCHEDULE DURATION
Total Steps 1 & 2. Scope/Organize	16	1	16
Total Step 3. Gather Information	8	12	12
Total Step 4. Develop the Blueprint	4	11	13
Total Step 5. Create Draft Materials	5	27	30
Total Step 6. Test Draft Materials	6	9	9
Total Step 7. Produce the Masters	8	21	27
Total Step 8. Reproduce	0	4	17
Total Step 9. Distribute	0	0	0
Total Step 10. Evaluate	0	0	0
GRAND TOTAL, ALL STEPS:	47	85	124

Arrgh! It's Going to Take Too Long!

At this point you might be saying to yourself, "How in the world am I going to sell a project to my sponsor when it requires so much time!?" Let's look at our example project; pay particular attention to the Summary Time Estimate. Here are some things to keep in mind:

Sponsor involvement with the project will likely begin with Step 3: Gather Information and end with Step 7: Produce the Masters. The sponsor will not be personally involved in the first 16 days of effort spent by you scoping and organizing the project and will likely be able to "go away" when production begins.

Courseware will be available for the first time at Step 6: Test Draft Materials. Some members of our training audience could be trained at this point by participating in this Test. (This is only about 75 days, or 60%, into the process — not 124 days as our full project time estimate indicates.)

Revised drafts of materials will be available about a week or so into Step 7: Produce the Masters. If necessary, some members of our training audience could be using "quick and dirty" photocopies of our drafts while the production and reproduction processes are underway. (This is about 85 days, or 68%, into the process — nearly 40 days less than the 124 days.)

As project manager, you want to ensure the creation of quality courseware by following a systematic development process. You can't afford shortcuts, nor do you necessarily have to take them. As shown above, if your sponsor demands minimum involvement and courseware available as quickly as possible, you can respond by pointing out two important facts:

- Sponsor involvement won't become substantial until Step 3: Gather Information. And throughout the project this involvement will take the form of critical intervention only (input/review/feedback), not daily participation.

- You can have training ready for some trainees as early as 60% of the way through the project.

Pointing out these facts should help you sell your project time estimate to a sponsor who "wants training yesterday."

Estimating Project Costs

So far, we have discussed how to estimate:

- The **amount of materials** needed for a course

- The **time** it will take to create those materials

These are the two prerequisites for making your estimate of project costs. Each of these must be factored in to the project budget. Before you try to create a project budget, however, you need to consider project costs in broad terms.

Two Types of Project Costs

Generally, there are two types of project costs: labor and outside purchases.

Labor Costs

Labor costs include the money paid for salaries and benefits for the people who work on the project. Usually, project managers and designers account for most labor costs on a project.

Outside Purchases

Outside purchases consist of goods and services that must be purchased in order to complete the project. The costs of outside purchases are usually fixed, as in a "fixed-price" contract provided by a vendor. Examples of outside purchases include:

- A contract with a producer to create a video tape

- A contract with an instructional development expert to complete a task analysis or to conduct an evaluation

- Typesetting services used to create master materials

- Graphics created by an outside artist

- Reproduction services

- Express mail charges for shipping materials to reviewers

- Catered meals for course participants during the test

You can probably think of many more examples. The important thing for now, however, is to be aware of outside purchases as one category of project costs.

Figuring Project Costs

It's fairly easy to figure project costs, once you have estimated the amount of materials required and the number of days needed to create

---

Number of Days X Daily Labor Costs = Project Labor Costs

Project Labor Costs
+ Outside Purchases
Total Project Costs

Figure 2-5: Figuring Project Costs

them. In ultra-simplified form, the process looks like this:

On the next page is a worksheet that can help. Note that it includes some rules of thumb, but for the most part you will need to research the specific prices paid by your organization for labor and outside purchases in your local area.

Worksheet: Estimating Project Costs

The following worksheet can be used to help you estimate project costs. Before you try to use this worksheet, **have the following on hand**:

● The worksheets *Estimating Materials Required* and *Estimating Project Time*, with all appropriate blanks filled in

● The average daily pay rate for a project manager and a designer in your organization (include benefits, if applicable)

● The average daily pay rate for a designer/developer (ID) in your area   (Typical rates are $400 to $600.)

● Any information about your project that could affect project costs, including:

— **Set up charges:** How much will it cost to set up the classroom environment and/or rent equipment or facilities?

— **Special print formats:** Do you require unusual formats for job aids or other handouts? Will special packaging, lamination, or other physical treatments of finished materials be required?

— **Reproduction method:** Will you be using photocopy or offset reproduction methods?

— **Distribution method:** Will you be distributing your course materials via ground or air shippers? ... via express or slower (and cheaper) methods?

When you have all these materials together, you are ready to begin your project cost estimate.

1. Determine Project Scope

Mgr.: _____ days X $ _____ daily rate = $ _____

ID: _____ days X $ _____ daily rate = $ _____

Other: _____ days X $ _____ daily rate = $ _____

Travel: $ _____

Communications/Shipping: $ _____

Duplication: $ _____

Catering: $ _____

Supplies: $ _____

Other: $ _____

Total Step 1: $ _____

2. Organize the Project

Mgr.: _____ days X $ _____ daily rate = $ _____

ID: _____ days X $ _____ daily rate = $ _____

Other: _____ days X $ _____ daily rate = $ _____

Travel: $ _____

Communications/Shipping: $ _____

Duplication: $ _____

Catering: $ _____

Supplies: $ _____

Equipment Rental: $ _____

Other: $ _____

Total Step 2: $ _____

3. Gather Information

Mgr.: _____ days X $ _____ daily rate = $ _____

ID: _____ days X $ _____ daily rate = $ _____

Vendor: _____ days X $ _____ daily rate = $ _____

Other: _____ days X $ _____ daily rate = $ _____

Other: _____ days X $ _____ daily rate = $ _____

Travel: $ _____

Communications/Shipping: $ _____

Duplication: $ _____

Catering: $ _____

Supplies: $ _____

Equipment Rental: $ _____

Other: $ _____

Total Step 3: $ _____

4. Develop the Blueprint

Mgr.: _____ days X $ _____ daily rate = $ _____

ID: _____ days X $ _____ daily rate = $ _____

Vendor: _____ days X $ _____ daily rate = $ _____

Other: _____ days X $ _____ daily rate = $ _____

Travel: $ _____

Communications/Shipping: $ _____

Duplication: $ _____

Catering: $ _____

Supplies: $ _____

Equipment Rental: $ _____

Other: $ _____

Total Step 4: $ _____

5. Create Draft Materials

Mgr.: _____ days X $ _____ daily rate = $ _____

ID: _____ days X $ _____ daily rate = $ _____

Vendor: _____ days X $ _____ daily rate = $ _____

Other: _____ days X $ _____ daily rate = $ _____

Travel: $ _____

Communications/Shipping: $ _____

Duplication: $ _____

Catering: $ _____

Supplies: $ _____

Equipment Rental: $ _____

Other: $ _____

Total Step 5 $ _____

6. Test Draft Materials

Mgr.: _____ days X $ _____ daily rate = $ _____

ID: _____ days X $ _____ daily rate = $ _____

Vendor: _____ days X $ _____ daily rate = $ _____

Trainer: _____ days X $ _____ daily rate = $ _____

Other: _____ days X $ _____ daily rate = $ _____

Travel: $ _____

Communications/Shipping: $ _____

Duplication: $ _____

Catering: $ _____

Supplies: $ _____

Equipment Rental: $ _____

Other: $ _____

Total Step 6: $ _____

7. Produce Master Materials

Mgr.: _____ days X $ _____ daily rate = $ _____

ID: _____ days X $ _____ daily rate = $ _____

Vendor: _____ days X $ _____ daily rate = $ _____

Other: _____ days X $ _____ daily rate = $ _____

Other: _____ days X $ _____ daily rate = $ _____

Travel: $ _____

Communications/Shipping: $ _____

Duplication: $ _____

Catering: $ _____

Supplies: $ _____

Video masters
($2 - 15K per minute*): $ _____

Overhead transparency masters: $ _____

35 mm slide masters: $ _____

Audio tape masters
($1 - 7K per minute*): $ _____

Graphics artwork
($20 - 200 per graphic*): $ _____

Print masters
($25 - 40 per page, typeset*): $ _____

Editorial services: $ _____

Spine and cover art: $ _____

Disk and tape label masters: $ _____

Other: $ _____

Other: $ _____

Total Step 7: $ _____

* The range in cost of this item is based on complexity and "flash," or production value required.

8. Reproduce

Mgr.: _____ days X $ _____ daily rate = $ _____

ID: _____ days X $ _____ daily rate = $ _____

Vendor: _____ days X $ _____ daily rate = $ _____

Other: _____ days X $ _____ daily rate = $ _____

Other: _____ days X $ _____ daily rate = $ _____

Travel: $ _____

Communications/Shipping: $ _____

Catering: $ _____

Supplies: $ _____

Equipment Rental: $ _____

Video copies: $ _____

Overhead transparency copies: $ _____

35 mm slide copies: $ _____

Audio tape copies: $ _____

Print copies: $ _____

Editorial/packaging/
assembly services: $ _____

Binders: $ _____

Computer Disks: $ _____

Spine and cover
art copies: $ _____

Disk and tape labels: $ _____

Other: $ _____

Other: $ _____

Other: $ _____

Other: $ _____

Total Step 8: $ _____

9. Distribute

Mgr.: _____ days X $ _____ daily rate = $ _____

ID: _____ days X $ _____ daily rate = $ _____

Vendor: _____ days X $ _____ daily rate = $ _____

Other: _____ days X $ _____ daily rate = $ _____

Travel: $ _____

Communications/Shipping: $ _____

Duplication: $ _____

Catering: $ _____

Supplies: $ _____

Equipment Rental: $ _____

Other: $ _____

Total Step 9: $ _____

10. Evaluate

Mgr.: _____ days X $ _____ daily rate = $ _____

ID: _____ days X $ _____ daily rate = $ _____

Vendor: _____ days X $ _____ daily rate = $ _____

Other: _____ days X $ _____ daily rate = $ _____

Travel: $ _____

Communications/Shipping: $ _____

Duplication: $ _____

Catering: $ _____

Supplies: $ _____

Equipment Rental: $ _____

Other: $ _____

Other: $ _____

Total Step 10: $ _____

To find the total cost of course development, transfer all the "Total Step..." costs from the preceding pages to the list below.

Total Costs

Step 1.   Determine Project Scope   _____

Step 2.   Organize the Project   _____

Step 3.   Gather Information   _____

Step 4.   Develop the Blueprint   _____

Step 5.   Create Draft Materials   _____

Step 6.   Test Draft Materials   _____

Step 7.   Produce Master Materials   _____

Step 8.   Reproduce   _____

Step 9.   Distribute   _____

Step 10.   Evaluate   _____

Total Estimated Costs: _____

10% Margin of Error: x 1.10*

GRAND TOTAL COST ESTIMATE: _____

* Use your judgment with this. You might want to go as high as 30% on a project that appears unstable or difficult to estimate and control. Consider complexity and stability of the content, potential SME or sponsor control problems, and your design team's level of experience.

Case Study Example 3: Estimating Project Costs

Now let's examine how you might use this worksheet to estimate costs for a particular development effort. In this example, we'll continue with the project from Case Study Examples 1 & 2. Here's the situation:

In the first two case studies, you figured out how many materials and how much time were required to create a one-day course. In this case study, you will estimate the cost of that project. So far you know the following:

- The in-house project manager who will work on this course earns about $75,000 a year, including benefits. At 220 working days a year, this amounts to roughly $340 a day.

- The vendor designer, an independent contractor, will be earning about $500 a day.

- You will involve the audio-visual vendor in planning meetings but you won't pay for this vendor service; the vendor will recover the costs in her fixed price contract.

- Audio and video productions will be moderately "flashy." They won't be mere talking heads and deadly narration, but they won't look and sound like Star Wars, either.

- All print materials will be mastered internally, at a cost of about $30 a page.

- Graphics for overheads and flip charts will be produced in-house at a cost of $35 a unit.

- Your internal Print Center will handle reproduction of print materials. After hearing the quantities you need and discussing packaging and binding, they quoted you a fixed price of $15,000 for reproduction.

- Video and audio reproduction will be handled by the audio-visual vendor. Since only a few extra copies of the materials will be needed, you estimate that this won't cost more than $200.

- Test participants will be drawn from the local branch, so no travel and living expenses will be incurred during the test.

Given this situation, we need to answer this question:
How much will it cost to complete this development effort?

Here's how your completed worksheet might look:

Solution to Case Study Number 3: Estimating Project Costs

1. Determine Project Scope   (Not applicable to this project.)

2. Organize the Project

Mgr.: ___16___ days X ___$340___ daily rate = ___$5,440___

ID: ___1___ days X ___$500___ daily rate = ___$ 500___

Other: _____ days X $ _____ daily rate = $_____

Travel: $_____

Communications/Shipping: $_____

Duplication: $_____

Catering: $_____

Supplies: $_____

Equipment Rental: $_____

Other: $_____

Total Step 2: **$5,940**

3. Gather Information

Mgr.: ___8___ days X ___$340___ daily rate = ___$2,720___

ID: ___12___ days X ___$500___ daily rate = ___$6,000___

Vendor: _____ days X $ _____ daily rate = $_____

Other: _____ days X $ _____ daily rate = $_____

Other: _____ days X $ _____ daily rate = $_____

Travel: $_____

Communications/Shipping: $ 100_____

Duplication/Catering: $ 100_____

Supplies/Equipment Rental: $_____

Total Step 3: **$8,920**

4. Develop the Blueprint

Mgr.: ___4___ days X ___$340___ daily rate = $1,360 _____

ID: ___11__ days X ___$500___ daily rate = $5,500 _____

Vendor: _____ days X $ _____ daily rate = $ _____

Other: _____ days X $ _____ daily rate = $ _____

Travel: $ _____

Communications/Shipping: $ 100 _____

Duplication: $ 100 _____

Catering: $ 100 _____

Supplies: $ _____

Equipment Rental: $ _____

Other: $ _____

Total Step 4: **$7,160** _____

5. Create Draft Materials

Mgr.: ___5___ days X ___$340___ daily rate = $ 1,700 _____

ID: ___27__ days X ___$500___ daily rate = $13,500 _____

Vendor: _____ days X $ _____ daily rate = $ _____

Other: _____ days X $ _____ daily rate = $ _____

Travel: $ _____

Communications/Shipping: $ 200 _____

Duplication: $ 200 _____

Catering: $ 200 _____

Supplies: $ _____

Equipment Rental: $ _____

Other: $ _____

Total Step 5 **$15,800** _____

6. Test Draft Materials

Mgr.: ___6___ days X ___$340___ daily rate = $2,040 _____

ID: ___9___ days X ___$500___ daily rate = $4,500 _____

Vendor: _____ days X $ _____ daily rate = $_____

Trainer: _____ days X $ _____ daily rate = $_____

Other: _____ days X $ _____ daily rate = $_____

Travel: $_____

Communications/Shipping: $ 100 _____

Duplication: $ 200 _____

Catering: $ 300 _____

Supplies: $_____

Equipment Rental: $_____

Other: $_____

Total Step 6: $7,140 _____

7. Produce Master Materials

Mgr.:   8   days X $340   daily rate = $ 2,720

ID: 21 days X $500   daily rate = $10,500

Vendor: _____ days X $ _____ daily rate = $ _____

Other: _____ days X $ _____ daily rate = $ _____

Other: _____ days X $ _____ daily rate = $ _____

Travel: $ _____

Communications/Shipping: $ 100

Duplication: $ 100

Catering: $ _____

Supplies: $ _____

Video masters
($2 - 15K per minute): $90,000

(18 min. X $5,000 = $90,000)

Overhead transparency masters: $ _____

35 mm slide masters: $ _____

Audio tape masters
($1 - 7K per minute): $12,500

(5 min. X $2,500 = $12,500)

Graphics artwork
($20 - 200 per graphic): $1,400

(40 units X $35 each = $1,400)

Print Masters
($25 - 40 per page, typeset): $6,000

*(243 - 43 [AV script pages] = 200;
200 X $30 = $6,000)*

Editorial services: $ _____

Spine and cover art: $ _____

Disk and tape label masters: $ _____

Total Step 7:   **$123,320**

8. Reproduce

Mgr.: _____ days X $ _____ daily rate = $_____

ID: __4__ days X __$500__ daily rate = $ 2,000 _____

Vendor: _____ days X $ _____ daily rate = $_____

Other: _____ days X $ _____ daily rate = $_____

Other: _____ days X $ _____ daily rate = $_____

Travel: $_____

Communications/Shipping: $_____

Catering: $_____

Supplies: $_____

Equipment Rental: $_____

Video copies: $ 200 _____

Overhead transparency copies: $_____

35 mm slide copies: $_____

Audio tape copies: $_____

Print copies: $15,000 _____

Editorial/packaging/
assembly services: $_____

Binders: $_____

Computer Disks: $_____

Spine and cover
art copies: $_____

Disk and tape labels: $_____

Other: $_____

Other: $_____

Other: $_____

Other: $_____

Total Step 8: $17,200 _____

9. Distribute

(Not applicable)

10. Evaluate

(Not applicable)

Cost Summary

To find the total cost of course development, transfer all the "Total Step..." costs from the preceding pages to the list below.

		Total Costs
Step 1.	Determine Project Scope	N/A
Step 2.	Organize the Project	$ 5,940
Step 3.	Gather Information	$ 8,920
Step 4.	Develop the Blueprint	$ 7,160
Step 5.	Create Draft Materials	$ 15,800
Step 6.	Test Draft Materials	$ 7,140
Step 7.	Produce Master Materials	$123,320
Step 8.	Reproduce	$ 17,200
Step 9.	Distribute	N/A
Step 10.	Evaluate	N/A
	Total Estimated Costs:	**$185,480**
	10% Margin of Error:	x 1.10
	GRAND TOTAL COST ESTIMATE:	**$204,028**

Arrgh! It's Going to Cost Too Much!

At this point you might be saying to yourself, "How can I sell a project to my sponsor when it costs so much!?" Let's think about our example project. Here are some things you and your sponsor might consider in order to save money.

- Could we reduce the amount of materials that need to be created? (For example, could we use existing documentation or text materials instead of researching and developing new materials?)

- Could we eliminate or trim down expensive media? (For example, could we use printed case studies instead of video presentations or could we use media that are less flashy?)

- Could we use fewer developers or developers who charge us less money? (For example, might subject matter experts participate in writing some materials or could student interns from a local Educational Technology program be employed?)

- Could we completely eliminate the costs of formal print production and reproduction by using desktop published and photocopied materials?

You can probably think of many other ways to save money on the project. However, it is important to your project "selling" effort that you involve your sponsor in helping you to "downsize" the project when you are trying to cut costs. Ask him or her to sit with you and go over your detailed estimates of deliverables, time, and costs, and help decide where you can make sacrifices. When you both agree on all the project assumptions, there will be a greater likelihood of a smooth and successful development effort.

Conclusion

This chapter has described how to complete Step 1 of the ID project management process, Determine Project Scope. It has shown how you can build fairly detailed estimates of required course materials, development time, and project costs. In addition, it has emphasized that materials estimates must precede time estimates and that time estimates must precede cost estimates. Finally, it has provided some worksheets and rules of thumb to help you in developing your own estimates of project scope.

A caution: We strongly urge you to find or develop rules of thumb that are unique to your organization and industry. In the long run, these will be more valuable than the generic tools presented here.

One final note: The project scoping activities described here can involve a lot of number crunching. This need not be a tedious job. There are lots of personal computer applications which can speed up and partially automate these estimating chores. Spreadsheet programs and even some databases can help. In addition, there are several good project management software products on the market that are specially designed for planning and tracking projects. These will not only support your cost-estimating efforts, but can also produce Gantt and PERT scheduling charts, work breakdown information, and lots of other valuable reports. If you are serious about your project management, you should spend some time at your local software store investigating these products. They can make a significant difference in helping you plan, control, and communicate with project team members.

Chapter 3

How to Organize the Project

In the first chapter we presented a 10-step project management model and an overview of the project manager's role in working within the model. In the second chapter we examined, in detail, Step 1: Determine Project Scope.

This chapter focuses on what you need to do after your estimates of project scope are approved by your sponsor and you are ready to begin the project. Specifically, this chapter will describe Step 2 of the project management process, Organize the Project.

Overview

There are four main activities in organizing the project. First, confirm that your original assumptions about the project are still valid. Next, assemble the project team and set up a diary to help you control project details. Finally, hold a Kickoff meeting to get the project off to a good start.

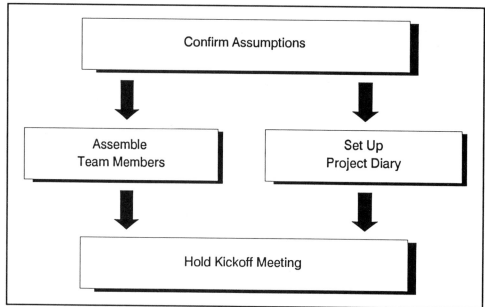

Figure 3-1: Major Activities in Organizing the Project

Let's examine each of these activities in detail.

Confirm Project Assumptions

It is often true that weeks or even months pass between the scoping of the project (Step 1) and the time when the project is "sold" or is approved to start. A lot of things can change as this time passes.

For example, the project manager who originally made the estimate of project scope may leave the company, along with the assumptions he or she used to plan the project. Or the project may gain a new sponsor (or worse, lose an old sponsor!). Or the trainees' job descriptions might change, necessitating new objectives, and ultimately new materials. And, finally, there are the inevitable changes made to course content as your plans are examined by decision-makers. Because of these possibilities, it is essential to confirm the scope of your project before you begin work. This way, you won't be trying to execute an outdated project plan. The following guidelines can help.

Guidelines for Confirming Project Assumptions

If substantial time has passed since you completed your estimates of project scope, you should confirm your assumptions before you start the project. These guidelines can help.

Step 1: The first thing to do is to find the course sponsor and review the course parameters. You need to **find out**:

☐ Are the general goals and objectives still on target? (Review these verbally with the sponsor.)

☐ Does the audience still consist of the same people? (You might ask the sponsor if you can make a quick phone call to a couple of audience members in order to get your bearings.)

☐ Is the content still the same? (Will there be anything new or anything that should be deleted?)

☐ Are the plans for marketing the product (or starting the program, or whatever) still the same? What has changed?

☐ Has the amount of money available for the training changed?

☐ Does the sponsor still support the training to the extent needed to provide necessary SMEs, documentation, and equipment?

☐ Are implementation plans still the same? (trainers required, dates, locations, etc?)

Step 2: If the answers above satisfy you, then you are ready to **review the project scope.** Review assumptions about:

☐ Materials required

☐ Time needed

☐ Project costs

> **Note: If there are no usable records of planned materials, time, or costs,** then you must create them at this point. You should come out of this review with detailed numbers, like those you would find in the three scoping worksheets discussed in the last chapter. If serious questions surface during your discussions with the sponsor or your review of project scope, don't hesitate to raise a red flag. It is better to rethink the project now, before time or money are expended, than to have to cancel it later, after wasting valuable time and resources.

Assemble the Project Team

An instructional development project is a complicated undertaking, sometimes involving as many as 15 or 20 people. On even the smallest projects, when each person may wear a couple of different hats, there are still six fundamental roles that must be played:

- **Sponsor** (sometimes called customer or client)
- **Subject Matter Expert** (SME)
- **Designer** (sometimes called instructional developer or ID)
- **Production Coordinator**
- **Trainer** (sometimes called instructor or facilitator)
- **Project Manager**

The people playing these roles must know their responsibilities and must be committed to executing them quickly and efficiently. As project manager, you must communicate these responsibilities at the beginning of the project, clarifying who does what for whom, when. The following tool is designed to help.

Who's Who on Your Project Team: A Reference Aid

How to Use This Reference Aid

Note that there are boxes to the left of each statement of responsibility. To figure out the roles and responsibilities required on your project, simply go through the list and place a check mark next to the ones that must be fulfilled. Later, you can pencil-in the initials of the specific person who will actually be given each responsibility. Alternately, you might pass out the role descriptions at the Kickoff meeting and confirm them with everyone at one time.

Sponsor

Definition: This is the person who is paying for the project and who has requested that the project be undertaken.

Responsibilities: Sponsor responsibilities typically include:

☐ Helps identify the training requirements and approves the project manager's preliminary project scope

☐ Specifies members of the target audience

☐ Helps other members of the team obtain access to the target audience during information gathering and testing of drafts

☐ Identifies sources of content (SMEs and/or documentation)

☐ Arranges for meetings between SMEs and designers

☐ Provides the organizational "clout" needed to get designers timely and accurate information about content and audience

☐ Provides funding for the training

☐ Reviews and approves initial project plans, design document, draft materials, test session, masters, and plans for reproduction and distribution

☐ Requests the support of SMEs or others to review the design document and drafts

☐ Gathers and synthesizes the comments of SMEs and other reviewers so that the designer is presented with a single, unified statement of required revisions and organizational policies related to the training

Subject Matter Expert (SME)

Definition:　This is the person who must take responsibility for the accuracy of the facts, concepts, and other content that will be presented. He or she does not necessarily know the most about these topics, but is able to make judgment calls when disputes concerning technical details arise.

Responsibilities:　SME responsibilities typically include:

- ☐ Provides the official "party line" about technical operation of equipment, essential facts that trainees must know, how these facts interrelate, product marketing goals, or specific tasks which trainees will perform on the job

- ☐ As the source of "official" approved content, bears the responsibility for accurate and timely information

- ☐ Reviews and approves the Blueprint and draft materials, especially noting technical inaccuracies

- ☐ Is available on a first priority basis for review and feedback with designers

Designer (instructional developer or ID)

Definition:　This is the person who performs consulting and development chores necessary to create instructional materials.

Responsibilities:　ID responsibilities typically include:

- ☐ Gathers and analyzes information about content and skills

- ☐ Determines performance objectives based on the results of information gathered

- ☐ Writes the Blueprint and draft materials

- ☐ Works with media people to assure that all master materials adhere to the design of the course

- ☐ Organizes the test session and rehearses the instructor

- ☐ Prepares the materials for the reviews required at each stage of the instructional development process

- ☐ Makes revisions specified by the project manager or sponsor

Production Coordinator

Definition: This is the person who must see to it that draft materials are transformed into master materials, suitable for reproduction. There may be one coordinator for each type of media required. (For example, you might have a print production coordinator, an audio production coordinator, a video production coordinator, and so on.)

Responsibilities: Typical Production Coordinator responsibilities include:

☐ Advises on "produceability" of design concepts at early stages of the development effort

☐ Provides suggestions on enhancing production values

☐ Manages and coordinates development of scripts

☐ Coordinates appropriate members of the production team after materials are approved for production

☐ Represents the reproduction people at early discussions regarding packaging, etc.

Trainer (instructor or facilitator)

Definition: This is the person who will be presenting the portions of the training that require lecture, facilitation, or other types of live coordination.

Responsibilities: Typical Trainer responsibilities include:

☐ Provides insight, based on teaching experience, on audience, instructional strategy, and delivery mechanisms

☐ Represents field delivery people in determining appropriate course logistics

☐ Reviews design document and drafts, especially noting training implementation and delivery issues

☐ Serves as instructor for test sessions and train-the-trainer sessions, attending rehearsals and planning meetings as needed

☐ Provides recommendations for course revisions based on reviews and test session results

Project Manager

Definition: This is the person who sees to it that the project team creates quality courseware on time and within budget.

Responsibilities: (For a detailed breakout of the manager's responsibilities [Steps 1 through 10] see "The Job of the Project Manager" in Part 1. Listed here are the broad, project-wide responsibilities only.)

Project Manager responsibilities typically include:

- ☐ Lays the groundwork for the development of cost-effective courseware by developing preliminary statements of project scope and confirming these with the sponsor

- ☐ Develops detailed plans for the overall "choreography" of the project elements throughout the development effort

- ☐ Hires or acquires the necessary designers and producers

- ☐ Supervises the designers and producers as they execute their responsibilities

- ☐ Eliminates roadblocks in the process by planning and anticipating difficulties and making frequent progress checks

- ☐ Assures that accepted instructional development standards and practices are followed throughout the project

- ☐ Assures that designers are getting necessary inputs from SMEs and sponsor

- ☐ Assures that the project is completed within the schedule and budget established

- ☐ Keeps the sponsor posted on deviations between the preliminary course specifications and the "real" course specifications as they evolve

- ☐ Keeps the sponsor aware of the need for additional resources so the sponsor can acquire them

- ☐ Regularly (every week or two) provides a written project status report to his or her management and to the sponsor

It's Okay to Combine Roles...Sometimes

The descriptions of responsibilities on the reference aid are neat and tidy. In the real world, however, you will probably have to combine some categories and separate others. For example, the sponsor may also serve as SME. Or the project manager may also wear the hat of the designer and production coordinator. In this case, however, we recommend that the project schedule be generous, since the "designer" will also be fighting his or her own political fires.

A word of caution: In most cases, SMEs should not try to serve as designers or developers of courseware. Because of their extensive familiarity with the content, SMEs often assume that learners know all sorts of information, both broad and detailed, which learners simply cannot know. Or worse, SMEs sometimes feel a need to provide far more technical detail than is warranted by the course objectives, simply because they are experts and enjoy sharing every aspect of their field. For these reasons, if SMEs must be used as designers or developers, the project manager should make certain to review their work carefully or have a trained ID provide thorough quality assurance and review of their outputs.

Find the Right SMEs

Keep these things in mind when choosing SMEs:

Avoid Incredible SMEs

It is important that any SMEs that you identify be credible in the eyes of the sponsor. If you intend to provide your own SMEs (by hiring outside consultants, for example), be sure you get the sponsor to approve those you choose. If you don't get this approval, you run the risk of allowing the sponsor to reject any or all of your courseware on the grounds that it is not technically accurate.

Make Sure SMEs Have First-hand Knowledge

Try to identify SMEs who are as close to the product or content as possible. SMEs who are working primarily from their assumptions or from theory instead of first-hand knowledge may provide inaccurate information. Worse, they could lead your designers to create exercises that seem ridiculous to trainees who actually perform the job every day.

Expect Your Sponsor to Filter SME Input

Make certain that the person who is approving the Blueprint and drafts (i.e., the sponsor) is the same person who will gather and filter comments from all SMEs and other reviewers. This way you or your designers can avoid being caught in the middle of disputes over the "right" technical details.

Hire the Right Designers

As you finalize your choice for designer, ask yourself:

- Is this designer truly available on a first priority, full-time basis for the duration of the project? If not, get someone who is.

- Does this designer have a solid track record in the training format required (CAI, gaming, interactive video, self-study text, etc.)?

- If appropriate, does this designer have experience developing training which includes technical content?

- Does this designer have good interviewing and client interface skills? (Remember that 80% of the typical project will involve consulting, as opposed to development of materials.)

- Because of his or her experience, could this designer serve as an early warning system by seeing and reporting project difficulties before they get out of hand?

Your choice of designer can make or break your project. So choose carefully!

Project Roles & Project Decision-Making

When managing the group of professionals that comprise the design team it is often difficult to assure that decisions are made efficiently. Typically, both the project manager and the sponsor will want to take advantage of the specialized training and unique job responsibilities of the professionals on the team. But what if these people disagree? For example, what if SMEs believe the training should start with a 20-minute lecture by one of their fellow SMEs, while the designer would like the training to start with a five-minute video-taped demonstration? Who casts the deciding vote?

Ultimately, it is the sponsor and the project manager who are responsible for seeing that the project results in what was promised by the initial project description. Therefore, recommendations should be funneled through the project manager and the sponsor. The diagram below illustrates how project decisions should be made.

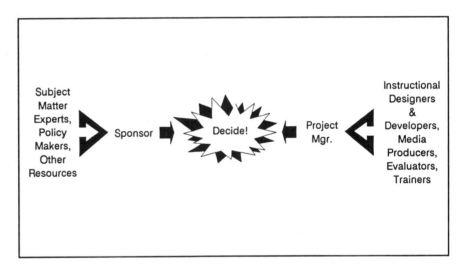

Figure 3-2: Project Decision-Making

Set Up the Project Diary

As you begin to organize your project, you are going to generate a lot of paperwork. That's where a project diary can help. Its purpose is to provide a single location where all essential project records can be found quickly and easily.

The project diary should be a three-ring binder with these sections:

- Proposal or Contract
- Materials Specifications
- Schedule
- Financial Information
- Vendor Contracts
- Project Status Reports
- Sign-off Forms
- Letters/Memos
- Conversations
- Subject Matter Experts
- Other Key People

The following guidelines describe each section in detail.

The Project Diary: Guidelines and Samples

Your project diary should be a one-stop source for all your project paperwork. It should be set up as a three-ring binder with these sections.

Proposal or Contract

This section should contain a copy of the written document that outlines the parts of the course, the materials required, the assumptions about audience and objectives, and any other agreements made between you and the sponsor.

If no such document exists, you should write a summary memo describing your understanding of these issues and send it to your supervisor and the sponsor when the project begins. Then place a copy here.

Materials Specifications

This section tells exactly what materials everyone has agreed to create. These should be expressed as specific numbers of pages of text, pages of job aids, minutes of audio-visual media, and so on. There should also be a description of the format of finished master materials and reproduction specifications. Materials estimation worksheets, completed during project planning, should be included.

Schedule

This should show the major milestones, review and sign-off points, deadlines for obtaining input from SMEs or vendors, and other important project dates. Be sure to note holidays, since these will affect the entire project team. You might include a PERT or Gantt chart for easy visualization.

The time requirements worksheets that you completed during preliminary project planning should also be kept here.

Financial Information

This section describes the funds allocated and lists any relevant purchase orders against which invoices should be charged. Cost estimating worksheets, completed earlier, should also be here.

Vendor Contracts

This section contains copies of contracts with all vendors.

Project Status Reports

This section contains short status reports (approx. 1 page) which are sent to project team members and upper management. Use bulletted lists of important comments, avoiding long, drawn-out explanations. Include all sections shown in this sample:

SAMPLE PROJECT STATUS REPORT:

Status Report: *XYZ Sales Training (Project No. XY768)*

Date: June 17, 19XX   **From:** Marcy Collins

Accomplishments: (Since June 10th report.)

- Began information gathering, which included calling technical SMEs and interviewing members of target audience

- Completed tracking down the first invoice from Zoomout Productions; determined an approximate date of payment

- Arranged for one XYZ model 17 system for the development team to be placed in the local branch for research purposes

Pending Items:

- Complete task analysis and revision of preliminary objectives

- Brainstorm with designers re: creative design strategies

- Start writing Blueprint

Concerns and Recommended Actions:

- Jim Rivers is recoiling at his proposed role as draft reviewer. Recommend using Martha Schwartz instead.

- Engineering still won't discuss the new parambulation attachment for the XYZ. We must get a demo and documentation by 6/23 or it will be dropped from the course.

Remarks:

- Many thanks to Earl Jordan for locating the missing XYZ marketing plans. This really helped us keep on our schedule.

The sign-off form is the document which the sponsor signs to indicate approval of a given project milestone. This document also indicates the sponsor's approval to proceed with the next step of the development cycle and to pay for this step, if applicable.

Sign-offs should be obtained after completion of the Blueprint, after completion of drafts, after the test, and after delivery of master materials. Use the sample below as a model.

SAMPLE SIGN-OFF FORM:

SIGN-OFF/APPROVAL OF BLUEPRINT

Project: *The Sales Rep's Guide to the XYZ*

I have reviewed and approved the Blueprint for the course named above, with changes, additions, deletions, or corrections, if any, as noted in the designer's master copy.

I hereby give the ID Department approval to proceed with creating the drafts of all workbooks, scripts, and other course materials. I also give my approval for the ID Department to invoice my department for satisfactory completion of the Blueprint milestone of this project.

I understand that further changes to the fundamental structure, objectives, or content of the course (aside from those changes specified in the designer's master Blueprint) will likely result in a slippage in the delivery date and could result in substantial additional charges to my department.

_____ *[signature]*

J. Edgar Casey, VP Marketing   *[sponsor's name]*

XYZ Supersystems, Inc.

Date: _____

cc:

Murphy Bridlow, ID Department Manager

Letters/Memos

This section contains letters or memos that relate to the project.

Conversations

This section is a written record of all important conversations (including phone calls) with key project players regarding the materials or controversial assumptions made about the course.

Promises from SMEs (like agreeing to send a particular document tomorrow) and other reviewers should be included. Each entry should be dated, with a brief description of the topic of conversation, the action required, and who initiated the conversation. *Here's a sample:*

Date:	Contact Name:	Summary of Talk:	Actions Items:
6/18	Bill Burton	Refused interview; said "not approved"	Call his boss, get approval

Subject Matter Experts

This section is organized by general categories of subject matter required for the course. Within each category it lists the name, address, and phone number of the person who can help provide information on the topic. *Here's a sample:*

Topic:	SME Name:	Phone Number:	Address:
Typical uses of the XYZ in hospitals	Jane Hunter	(213) 555-1324	Los Angeles
Marketing plan for XYZ	Tim Murray	(716) 555-9876	3380 Palm St. Ferndale, CA 90080

Other Key People

This section lists the names, addresses, phone numbers, and major responsibilities of each person associated with the project. It should also include administrative assistants who can "track down" the key person and organization charts, if possible.

Two Powerful Tools

The Project Diary guidelines include descriptions of several powerful tools that deserve to be highlighted. These are the project status report and the sign-off form.

The Project Status Report

As project manager you must attempt to manage a sometimes large and unwieldy team of professionals. To do so, you must keep in constant touch with them about their roles and responsibilities, your expectations, and any changes in the project. The project status report will help you keep everyone informed. In fact, since you will need to do a brief status check with every project team member in order to write the report, by simply putting the report together, you will benefit. What's more, the report can serve as an "official" forum to document important project decisions. In this way, should a sponsor or SME try to change project specifications mid-stream, you will have written documentation of decisions made.

Study the sample status report in the guidelines carefully and imagine how such a report might help you on your next project.

The Sign-off Form

Instructional development projects are finite; that is, they take a limited amount of time and money and result in a limited set of deliverables. On the other hand, the imaginations of the people on the ID project team are nearly infinite in scope; that is, our ID team can imagine all sorts of different instructional media and activities to accomplish the same instructional goals. Without an externally imposed discipline, such as the sign-off and approval process, the courseware would constantly be taking on new attributes. For example, what begins as a one-day instructor-led workshop could end up as a two-day workshop with a video-based, one-day self-study pre-school kit. As we have seen in Chapter 2, the time and resources required to create these different instructional approaches will likely vary a great deal.

As project manager, you make a commitment to your sponsor to build a specific set of materials, within a specific time-frame, using a specific amount of resources (money, people, etc.). The sign-off process prevents the project team (including the sponsor and SMEs) from undermining this commitment by constantly changing their minds.

As the sample shows, when your sponsor approves a specific project milestone, he or she also acknowledges that it will probably cost more and/or require a schedule extension to change his or her mind later. In this way, the sign-off process can help you live within your budget and schedule.

Hold the Kickoff Meeting

Up to this point, you have been operating behind the scenes, creating the plans and tools that will help you achieve a successful project. Now it's time to get your team involved by holding a Kickoff meeting.

The project Kickoff meeting is the first formal meeting of all members of the project team. The **meeting has these purposes:**

- To clarify materials to be created

- To clarify roles and responsibilities

- To create a feeling of common purpose among team members

- To get each team member's commitment to perform his or her tasks according to specific dates

- To make certain that all team members have what they need to "hit the ground running" when the meeting is over

There is no meeting that is more important to the overall project success than the Kickoff meeting. The guidelines that follow provide some hints on how each of the meeting's purposes can be achieved.

Planning the Kickoff Meeting

The following guidelines can be used to help you plan your project kickoff meeting.

Clarify Materials to Be Created

Each member of the project team should have a clear, concrete image of what will be created at each stage of the development process. To clarify the materials that must be created, the project manager should:

- Review the development process (steps and outputs of each stage)

- Review a list of specific materials to be created:

    - Pages of Blueprint

    - Pages of workbook, instructor notes, scripts, and other materials

- Show examples of the outputs of each step in the process

- Show a sample Blueprint, highlighting key features

- Show samples of instructional materials that are similar to the ones that the team will be creating

In this way, everyone will know what results the development process will be geared to accomplish. They will also have an opportunity to suggest alternatives, if they strongly disagree.

Clarify Roles and Responsibilities

A development project is similar to a stage play in that the movements of each of the players must be carefully choreographed. At any given time, one member of the project team will be creating output that will serve as another person's input. If the project is to run smoothly, everyone must know what everyone else will be doing at each step of the process.

To clarify roles and responsibilities, the project manager should:

- Refer to the reference aid "The Project Team." Fill in the initials of a specific team member beside each statement of responsibility.

- At the Kickoff meeting, review all team members' responsibilities. Make sure that:

  - Each person agrees to his or her responsibilities by publicly stating that agreement

  - Each person understands what everyone else will be doing, especially: 1) who will be providing input at specific times, and 2) to whom his or her output must go at specific times

One Trap to Avoid

The Kickoff meeting, like any business meeting, can involve some jockeying for position among those attending. Some people will try to define their roles so that they do as little as possible. The project manager must be wary of this behavior and stick to his or her definitions of responsibilities. Agreements should be made openly, then documented in summary form after the meeting.

One common trap that project managers fall into is accepting responsibility to find or create course content. This often happens when a powerful sponsor or SME convinces the team that he or she is too busy to provide some parts of the required content.

Be forewarned: **It is usually a waste of time for the project manager or designer to search for or create content.** The sponsor is not only in a better position to find the right content in the first place, but he or she is ultimately going to pass judgment on the suitability of anything the manager or designer uncovers. Specific referrals by the sponsor to documentation (including specific publication name, location, etc.) are acceptable. **It is preferred, however, that the sponsor or his/her delegated SME locate and screen all content.** There is an analogy here that may clarify the situation. The writer of the corporate report does not invent policy statements or financial figures, he or she simply molds this information into a polished report. In a similar way, instructional designers do not create content, but rather they shape and mold content to create training.

Create a Feeling of Common Purpose

The project Kickoff meeting has a strong element of ritual associated with it. It is the time to give everyone the feeling that what he or she is doing is special, yet is contributing to a larger purpose. It is also when the team really begins to become a team.

It is a good idea for the project manager to show how the course to be developed fits within the larger curriculum, then relate the larger curriculum to the overall corporate strategies. This will help people on the team to feel that their contribution will really make a difference.

It is also important for the manager to spend enough time introducing each team member to establish his or her credibility in the eyes of the others. List each person's past successes and describe, in detail, what skills the person brings to the project. Make it clear that you are convinced the person is the best person for the job. In this way, the project manager can help establish an atmosphere of mutual respect.

Finally, and most importantly, the project manager should **get excited about the project and share that excitement!** In the weeks and months ahead, the energy of this enthusiasm can help carry the team through long hours of frustration and hard work.

At the Kickoff meeting the project manager should be prepared to get commitment to specific calendar dates for the completion of activities by each team member.

To accomplish this goal, however, the project manager should have prepared a specific calendar ahead of time. This way, the meeting will simply involve confirming or modifying dates, instead of trying to invent them on the spot.

To prepare your calendar before the meeting, **assemble the following:**

● Your completed worksheet, Estimating Time Needed

● A calendar listing national and company holidays

● A list of vacation dates for the people on the project team

When you have these things together, **complete a schedule similar to this sample:**

Worksheet: The Project Calendar

STEP:	DATE:	PERSON:	NOTES:

Step 2. Organize the Project

Complete planning _____ _____ _____

Hold Kickoff meeting * _____ _____ _____

Step 3. Gather Information

Plan/strategize _____ _____ _____

Complete analysis _____ _____ _____

Complete content review * _____ _____ _____

Step 4. Develop the Blueprint

Brainstorm/strategize _____ _____ _____

Complete Blueprint, give to proj. mgr. for review _____ _____ _____

Project mgr. review w/ designer _____ _____ _____

Complete revisions, present to sponsors, SMEs _____ _____ _____

Sponsors, SMEs review with designer and proj. mgr. * _____ _____ _____

Step 5. Create Draft Materials

Brainstorm/strategize _____ _____ _____

Proj. mgr. reviews sample pages, approves _____ _____ _____

Complete document, give to proj. mgr. for review _____ _____ _____

Proj. mgr. review with designer _____ _____ _____

Complete revisions, present to sponsors, SMEs _____ _____ _____

Sponsors, SMEs review with designer and proj. mgr. * _____ _____ _____

STEP:	DATE:	PERSON:	NOTES:

Step 6. Test Draft Materials

Complete revisions and
making copies

Complete set-up of classroom

Complete rehearsal with
instructor

Start the test session *

Complete the test session *

Complete debriefing session,
specify revisions *

Step 7. Produce Master Materials

Complete revisions

Complete copy editing

Complete pre-production
meeting with producers

Review sample print materials,
packaging plans

Attend video shoot

Attend audio recording

Attend video editing

Attend audio editing

Complete preparation for
sponsor review of masters

Complete sponsor review of
masters *

Complete revisions as specified
by sponsor

Deliver finished masters *

STEP:	DATE:	PERSON:	NOTES:

Step 8. Reproduce

Meet with reproduction vendor _____ _____ _____

Examine samples, approve _____ _____ _____

Complete reproduction * _____ _____ _____

Step 9. Distribute

Meet with distribution people
and plan _____ _____ _____

Complete distribution to field
locations * _____ _____ _____

---

* Note: To create an "Executive Overview" of the schedule for top
managers, include only these dates.

Make Certain That Team Members Have What They Need

At the end of the Kickoff meeting, each team member should have several specific action items and corresponding deadlines. Each project will require many different things that people will need in order to get started. The project manager should plan to have as many of these available as possible.

Here are some of the more important things that team members typically need immediately after the Kickoff meeting:

Sponsor Needs

Sponsors typically require detailed requests describing the things the team will need to complete the analysis. These include requests for:

- Approval to talk to customers, managers, and members of the target audience

- Specific appointments to see these people (the sponsor is usually the only one with enough "clout" to set these appointments in a timely manner)

- Access to confidential records, corporate plans, or new product details

After a Kickoff meeting, sponsors and SMEs often will need:

● Requests for demonstrations of products or processes

● Detailed requests for documentation

To help sponsors and SMEs provide content in the most useful format possible, consider giving them these guidelines:

SAMPLE GUIDELINES FOR SMEs:

HOW TO PROVIDE DOCUMENTATION

Good formats for providing information to designers or scriptwriters include:

● One page summaries

● Labels (yellow "stickies") to direct attention to important areas

● Labels to indicate whether the documentation is about to become obsolete

● Labels on each section telling whether it is very important, somewhat important, or nice-to-know

● Verbal walk-throughs of materials, using analogies to describe complex information

● Visually-oriented materials (overheads, diagrams, charts)

● Emphasizing any unique "angles" that will be used to help sell the product to sponsors or dealers (as long as they are accurate)

Bad formats for providing information include:

● An unlabeled pile of paper in the spirit of "You're on your own, pal!"

● Materials written by technical people, for technical people

● Segments taken out of context without explaining (verbally or in writing) the context

---

Designer Needs

To help designers get "up to speed" quickly after the Kickoff meeting, plan to provide them:

- Preliminary performance objectives

- All documentation that the project manager used to scope the course

- Samples of Blueprint and all course materials (to clarify format)

- Approval to see appropriate people and to use needed resources to get started (computer equipment, clerical support, etc.)

Production Coordinator Needs

To get your production coordinators up and running quickly, plan to provide them:

- Samples of particular media that could serve as models

- Approval to attend appropriate information gathering sessions to get the "feel" of the content or audience

- Appropriate documentation to help build script treatments or sample page layouts

When all the team members have what they need to get started, they will be able to "hit the ground running" after the Kickoff meeting. In short, the project manager will have planned for a successful development effort.

Conclusion

This chapter has described how to complete each of the four main activities in organizing the project. First, it reviewed how to confirm that your original assumptions about the project are still valid. Next, it described how to assemble the project team and set up a project diary. Finally, it described how to hold a Kickoff meeting to get the project off to a good start.

The next chapter will describe how to complete Step 3 of the ID project management process, Gather Information. It will answer the question "How can I be sure that my design team gets all the information it needs to create course materials?"

Chapter 4

How to Gather Information

In the first chapter, we presented a typical ID project management model and an overview of the project manager's job in implementing the model. The next two chapters provided information on Phase I of the model, Project Planning. Specifically, we presented techniques for completing Step 1: Determine Project Scope and Step 2: Organize the Project.

In this chapter, our focus will shift to Phase II: Instructional Development. (See Figure 1, on the next page.)

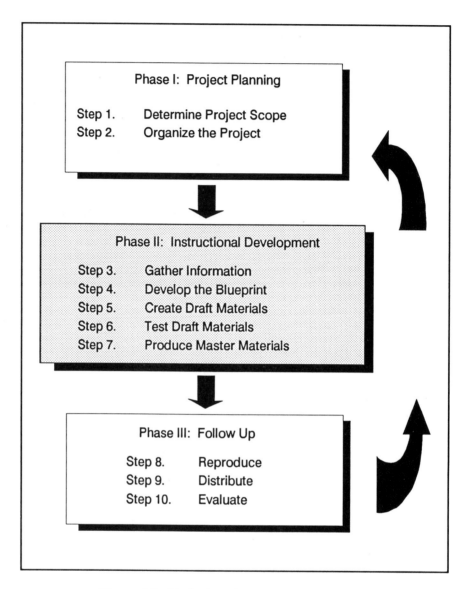

Figure 4-1: Typical Project Management Model

In this phase of the project, the manager's role changes. In Phase I: Project Planning, the manager performed most of the tasks for him- or herself. During Phase II, on the other hand, the manager will be coordinating the efforts of the members of the design team.

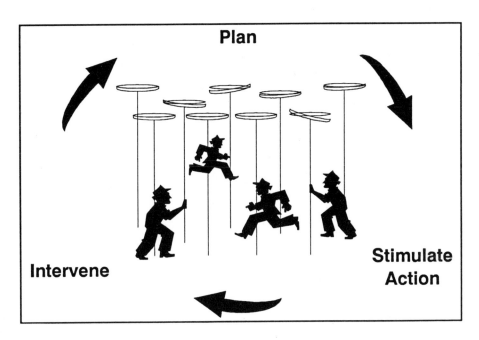

Plan

Intervene

Stimulate Action

Figure 4-2: Main Activities of a Project Manager

As the first chapter pointed out, to be a successful project manager you don't need to be directly involved in all the events that take place during a project. You must, however, carefully plan each event, provide the stimulus to get the event started, and then intervene when needed to keep things running smoothly. (Remember the plate-spinning analogy?) Figure 2 illustrates this process.

In this chapter we will review some techniques which will help you plan, stimulate action, and intervene as needed during Step 3: Gather Information.

Overview of Step 3: Gather Information

In this book we have drawn a distinction between front-end analysis and instructional development. To be specific, we assume that you must complete your front-end analysis (needs assessment, job analysis, performance analysis, or other preliminary analysis) before you try to plan an instructional development project. In other words, when you enter the model at Phase I, you are certain you have a need for training and that you have defined the nature of that need.

The purpose of Step 3: Gather Information is to get more details about the needed training so that designers can begin the instructional design process. Typically, your team will need to **gather detailed information about:**

- The **audience** to be trained

- The **tasks** the audience must learn to perform

- The **content**, or details, concerning the product or process on which the training will be based

Your first source of information on each of these topics should be the reports which resulted from your front-end analyses. These reports should be carefully reviewed to make sure your designers don't waste their time (or the sponsor's time) trying to gather information that is already available. After you have reviewed these reports, you will be ready to plan your information gathering to fill in the gaps.

While it is possible to make finer distinctions, there are basically **three broad sources of information** that training developers use:

- Observations

- Interviews

- Reviews of documentation

The table on the next page shows just a few examples of the ways these sources can be used to obtain different kinds of information.

Type of Information	Source of Information		
	Observations	Interviews	Documentation
Audience	Observe in work environment	Interview audience or supervisors	Employee files or personnel records
Tasks	Observe audience or expert performing	Interview expert or other performers	Job descriptions Policy statements Trouble reports
Content	Observe expert or creators of product/process	Interview SMEs, policymakers, marketers, or managers	Product plans Specifications Marketing guidelines

Figure 4-3: Examples of Information Gathering Techniques

It is not our intent here to discuss all possible information gathering techniques. There are plenty of good references (indeed, entire courses) devoted to these techniques. Consult these for details.

Planning to Gather Information

Usually the first task that your design team tries to perform together is Step 3: Gather Information. At this early stage, designers are just getting acquainted with each other and with the project; SMEs are rushing around trying to find documentation and prepare for interviews; and you are trying to make sure everyone is in the right place at the right time. Things can get pretty hectic.

Careful planning, however, can keep things running smoothly. While it can be valuable to involve your designers, it is still your responsibility as project manager to take the lead in this planning. Your planning should include these activities:

- Figure out, in broad terms, what information is missing.

- Pick one or more information gathering strategies that fit your schedule and budget.

- Tighten and polish your strategy.

The following worksheets and checklists can help.

Worksheet: What Information Is Missing?

To figure out, in broad terms, what kinds of information you need to gather, complete these steps.

Step 1: Assemble and review your project plans (proposal, budget, schedule, assumptions, etc.) and any documentation you have acquired concerning audience, tasks, or content.

Step 2: Try to "picture," or imagine in detail, the finished training materials you will be developing.

Step 3: Ask yourself "Which elements of the training will require more information before we can begin development?"

Step 4: In the spaces below, list the kinds of information you need to gather about the audience, the tasks they will be learning to perform, and the content (details) of the product or process they will be learning. **(List broad categories only.)**

Missing Information About the Audience

_____

_____

_____

_____

Missing Information About the Tasks to Be Performed

_____

_____

_____

_____

Missing Information About the Content
(details about the product/process)

_____

_____

_____

_____

Checklist: Potential Information Gathering Strategies

After you have completed the "Missing Information" worksheet, you are ready to identify some information gathering strategies. Review your list of missing information, then place a check mark beside the possible strategies you might use. (This is not an exhaustive list of strategies, by any means. Add your own strategies as required.)

Observations

Information on the Target Audience

- ☐ Observe them performing their job in the work environment
- ☐ Observe them interacting with people who provide inputs or people to whom they provide outputs
- ☐ Other:_____

Information on the Task

- ☐ Observe expert performing task (may be a narrated demonstration, with steps, substeps, and assumptions detailed)
- ☐ (If appropriate) Arrange for designer to perform the task, under supervision of an expert
- ☐ Other:_____

Information on the Product or Process

Observe inventor, designer, or initiator demonstrating how it works

Observe members of target audience using (or trying to use) the new product or process

Other:_____

Interviews

Information on the Target Audience

☐ Hold face-to-face or telephone interviews with members of the audience, their supervisors, their support people, etc.

☐ Ask inventors, designers, or initiators of the product or process their assumptions about the audience

☐ Other:_____

Information on the Task

☐ Interview inventors, designers, or initiators and ask about tasks, subtasks, assumptions regarding required skills

☐ Interview managers of training audience about criteria for successful performance (evaluative criteria or standards)

☐ Other:_____

Information on the Product or Process

☐ Interview inventors, designers, or initiators

☐ Interview promoters or marketing people "pushing" the product or process

☐ Interview managers or implementors of the product or process

☐ Other:_____

Review of Documentation

Information on the Target Audience

- ☐ Job descriptions
- ☐ Performance evaluation criteria, standards
- ☐ Requests for new staff member(s)
- ☐ Internal memos about meeting quotas, achieving expectations, etc.
- ☐ Other:_____

Information on the Task

- ☐ Detailed descriptions of steps of product or process to be performed
- ☐ Other:_____

Information on the Product or Process

- ☐ Technical specifications
- ☐ Position papers or memos advocating adoption of product or process
- ☐ Information on similar products or processes used by competitors
- ☐ User manuals, guidelines
- ☐ Marketing brochures
- ☐ Existing courseware for this or similar products or processes
- ☐ Other:_____

Worksheet: Tightening Your Information Gathering Strategy

After you have completed the "Potential Information Gathering Strategies" checklist you will have identified several strategies you want to use. There's a good chance, however, that you won't be able to do everything you would like to do. To narrow your strategies to a manageable number, complete these steps.

Step 1: Check your budget and schedule. Answer this: How much time and money are available for information gathering?

Time available: _____

Money available: _____

Step 2: Review your completed "Potential Information Gathering Strategies" checklist. Answer these questions:

How long will it take to prepare the interview questions, observation guidelines, and other tools that are needed to use the strategies you have identified?

_____

How long will it take to conduct the information gathering sessions?

_____

Will there be any outside costs (travel, consultants, equipment rental, etc.) that are not budgeted for? If so, how much extra costs are required?

_____

Step 3: Return to your "Potential Information Gathering Strategies" checklist and eliminate the strategies that fall outside your budget and schedule parameters.

Step 4: Review the remaining strategies and make a list of tools that are needed to implement them. (Observation guidelines, interview questionnaires, etc.)

When you have completed these worksheets, you will be ready to start gathering information.

Stimulating Action

After you have tightened your information gathering strategy, you are ready to put your designers to work implementing the strategy. (If time allows, you may want to have your designers review your strategy and then modify it based on their feedback.)

While the detailed activities will differ from project to project, you should **assign these general responsibilities to designers.**

- Develop guidelines, questionnaires, and other tools to be used during interviews and observations.

- Schedule and conduct observation sessions, meetings with interviewees, and meetings with SMEs for obtaining and reviewing documentation. (These might require an introductory phone call or letter from your sponsor, depending on the rank of the person with whom you are trying to meet.)

- Compare information gathered to information that is required, taking care to fill in all missing gaps.

- Verify that performance objectives, as specified in the original project plans, are still valid.

- Notify you immediately if it appears objectives or design strategy must be modified in any fundamental way.

Each of these general responsibilities should be assigned to a designer. As in any management situation, at the time you assign the responsibility you should provide as much detail as possible about your expectations, the resources available, and the deadline.

Once you make the assignment, however, all you can do is get out of the designer's way and keep an eye out for problems requiring your intervention.

Intervening

If you are lucky, and you have experienced designers working for you, you may have little need to intervene during information gathering. However, there are a few things you should watch out for no matter how smoothly the project seems to be going.

The following guidelines can help.

Intervention Guidelines: Gathering Information

This set of guidelines describes some typical interventions and inspections you might want to make during information gathering.

Daily Checks

Every day or so, check with each designer who is gathering information to **find answers to these questions:**

1. **Are people keeping their appointments** as scheduled? (SMEs, members of the target audience, other interviewees)

    If not, you should contact your sponsor and get him or her to "pull rank" or use some form of leverage to assure their involvement.

2. **Are you getting enough information** about the audience, the tasks they must perform, and the product or process to be trained?

    If not, figure out what the roadblocks are and take necessary steps to clear them. Get the sponsor involved in helping you, if necessary. Remember, time is money — so act quickly!

    If you are really stuck, you may want to quickly work through the planning worksheets again and revise your strategy.

3. **Are interviewees, SMEs, or others** with whom designers are meeting becoming **frustrated** or feeling their time is wasted?

    If so, you may need to spend some "public relations" time listening to them and selling them on the value of the project. In particular, point out how their contributions will provide long-term benefits in improving performance of the work force. To SMEs, you might want to point out that when the training program is installed, there will likely be fewer interruptions in their work to answer questions from novices.

    You should also check to see that designers are showing enthusiasm for the project. By showing their excitement about the project, they may stimulate SMEs or others to "get on board."

    Finally, check to see that designers are executing the information gathering strategy in an efficient manner. There is always the chance that they really are wasting time by using inefficient techniques.

4. **Are designers becoming overwhelmed** or bogged down in details? (Is panic setting in?)

If you detect signs of a designer becoming overloaded, meet with him or her and do the following:

☐ Ask the designer to review with you the performance objectives and the overall flow of the intended training.

☐ Ask the designer to describe how the information he or she is gathering fits in with the objectives and overall flow.

☐ Ask the designer to draw you a diagram of how all the details "fit together." Try to get him or her to stand back and look at the big picture, seeing the relationship of parts to the whole.

☐ If appropriate, remind the designer that the project will include lots of review by SMEs and opportunities for revision, so it isn't essential that he or she fully comprehend every minute detail at this point.

☐ Above all, show your confidence in the designer's abilities and demonstrate a sense of adventure in the discovery of the new information. Try to get the fun back in the process!

If information gathering is scheduled to run for a long time, you might want to check that the overloaded designer is getting enough time away from the project. If appropriate, suggest that he or she take a break or get involved in some kind of non-intellectual activity for a while.

About Two-Thirds of the Way Through...

About **two thirds of the way through** the information gathering cycle, **perform these activities:**

1. Review your original plans, proposals, and training descriptions.

2. Ask the designers to examine the original training objectives and course description and compare them with what they are learning during information gathering. Discuss their findings.

3. Note ways in which your original plans have become inappropriate.

4. Document the impact on the budget, schedule, or training implementation strategy.

5. Discuss these issues with the sponsor. Decide how to modify your plans.

Conclusion

This chapter has described some techniques for completing Step 3 of our ID project management model, Gather Information. First, we provided an overview of the instructional development information gathering process, distinguishing it from separate front-end analyses. Next, we reviewed some specific procedures for planning to gather information. In addition, we discussed how you might stimulate action by assigning particular activities to designers. Finally, we provided some guidelines for intervening during information gathering in order to make certain the project stays on track.

The next chapter will describe how to complete Step 4 of the ID project management process, Develop the Blueprint. It will answer the question "How can we create the best possible design specifications and organize them into a Blueprint for the training?"

Chapter 5

How to Develop the Blueprint

In the first three chapters of this book we presented a typical ID project management model, an overview of the project manager's job in implementing the model, and some techniques for completing Step 1: Determine Project Scope and Step 2: Organize the Project. In the preceding chapter, we reviewed some techniques to help you plan, stimulate action, and intervene as needed during Step 3: Gather Information.

This chapter describes how to manage Step 4: Develop the Blueprint.

What's a Blueprint?

If you have been developing training for any length of time, you have probably seen a blueprint or its equivalent. Sometimes called "design document," "design plans," or "design specifications," the blueprint plays an essential role in the development process.

A blueprint consists of these parts:

- **A "big picture" description of the instructional materials and course flow**, including how the materials fit into the larger curriculum. Course goals, audience background, and other general information are often included here.

- **A listing of specific performance objectives** to be attained by students. These should be presented in sequence, with enabling or sub-objectives identified.

- **A description of the instructional strategies** to be employed to attain each objective. This is essentially the "course choreography"; that is, a description of how learners will be presented with content and what they will be asked to do to practice applying this content.

- **A detailed outline of content** to be included in support of each objective. This outline should be in the form of bulletted lists of the facts, concepts, and other details for review and confirmation by SMEs. It should not be in prose form; rather, it should simply be in the form of a list.

- **A summary of media and materials** to be created to support each objective. For example, listed here are the number of pages of text, number of job aids, minutes of video, etc.

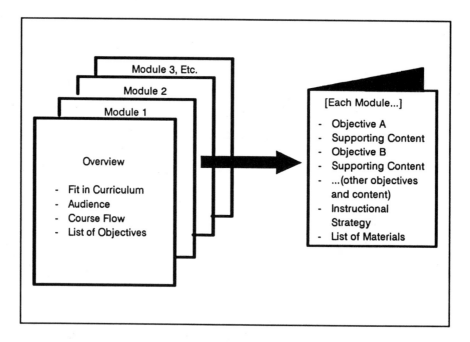

Figure 5-1: Blueprint Components

Why Bother Developing a Blueprint?

Many course sponsors and some novice project managers often ask, "Why bother with a blueprint? Why not just start writing instructional materials?"

The answer is simple: In the long run, developing a blueprint will save time and help you produce higher quality training materials. Here's why:

Viewed metaphorically, the blueprint is like a pile of bricks, not yet cemented together into a wall. The bricklayer is free to examine each brick on its own merit and throw it out or touch it up before the wall is built. After the wall is built, with mortar and trim in place, it is difficult and costly to change any of the bricks.

So it is with instructional materials. The objectives and content elements (i.e., the bricks) are easy to change when they are in outline form in the blueprint. After the instructional materials are created, complete with written introductions, transitions, exercises, job aids, and other materials (i.e., the mortar), it is costly and time consuming to change content or objectives. The slightest changes in content invariably "ripple through" all the materials.

By developing a blueprint you allow all reviewers to look at course content and strategy at a point when it is still malleable — before a lot of time and energy is expended. This early review encourages the design team to make meaningful revisions without the risk of damaging materials in which they have made substantial professional, emotional, or time investments. So in addition to saving money and time, you create an atmosphere in which members of the project team (SMEs, sponsors, designers) are able to discuss and rethink their strategies with less risk. In this way, you take advantage of everyone's expertise and help to create quality training.

Your Role as Manager

During the preceding step of the development process, Gather Information, your design team obtained detailed information about the training audience, the tasks which the audience must learn to perform, and the content of the training. What's more, before the project started, you made a commitment to your sponsor that you would create a certain set of materials within a particular budget and timeframe. As project manager, it's your job to see that the blueprint incorporates the new insights your team gained during Gather Information, yet at the same time respects your original commitments to the sponsor. This is not an easy balance to achieve. However, by completing the activities below, you ought to come close.

Here's what to do:

- Brainstorm about instructional strategies.

- Develop the blueprint.

- Quality Assure (QA) the blueprint and revise it if needed.

- Distribute the blueprint to reviewers.

- Obtain reviewer feedback and sponsor signoff.

To complete these you will need to plan carefully, stimulate the right action at the right time, and intervene intelligently. The following chart summarizes this process.

Manager Role / Activity	Plan	Stimulate Action	Intervene
Brainstorm	Review budget and schedule Review alternatives	Discuss instructional alternatives	Reduce alternatives to a realistic few
Develop the Blueprint	Find or make examples of blueprint	Share examples with designers; Set deadlines	Examine samples of each ID's blueprint
Quality-Assure	Assemble QA criteria	Get blueprint from each ID and QA	Provide feedback
Distribute to Reviewers	Prepare sponsor and SMEs	Send blueprint and provide guidelines for review	Call and check progress
Obtain Feedback and Signoff	Set up meeting for feedback	Start meeting; Review blueprint page by page	Keep team focused; Obtain signoff

Figure 5-2: Manager Activities During Develop the Blueprint

Now let's take a closer look at each of the manager's activities.

Brainstorm Instructional Strategies

The last activity that your design team completed was to Gather Information. During this step, they talked to SMEs, members of the target audience, and others to learn more about the real training need. At this point, therefore, your designers are likely to know more about the details of the training than you or your sponsor did when you made your project plans. In order to take advantage of this new information and capitalize on your designers' expertise, you should hold a brainstorming session.

You should plan the brainstorming session by preparing yourself to manage your designers' creativity. In particular, take a few moments and review your budget and schedule. These are your boundaries. You will not be able to exceed these without justification. So before you brainstorm with designers about alternatives, make sure you have the budget and schedule firmly in mind.

Next, review some instructional alternatives. If the course is likely to change as a result of what designers learned when they gathered information, what are some instructional alternatives that might fit your budget and schedule? Most basic textbooks on instructional design provide matrices or charts which compare instructional strategies. You might want to review some of these to help you recall the strengths and weaknesses of various approaches. After you have prepared yourself, you are ready to meet with your designers.

To get things started at the brainstorming session, you might list all the major objectives of the training. Then ask designers "Given what we learned when talking to SMEs or the target audience, what needs to be changed?" Or you might ask "If we had all the money and all the time we needed, what would be the very best training we could build?"

List as many alternatives as you can. Eventually, you will need to stop brainstorming and reduce your list of alternatives to the ones that will fit your budget and schedule. The exercise will be worthwhile, however, if it results in even one or two valuable new ideas.

Develop the Blueprint

After you have thoroughly discussed your alternatives, you are ready to develop the blueprint. Before you begin, however, you should provide designers with an example of any recommended blueprint format. Designers are creative people; if you don't share your format with them before they begin, they will probably invent their own. Your example should specify method of outlining, required sections of the blueprint, page layout, and so on.

You should then share this example blueprint with the designers, making sure they understand how it works. If someone suggests an improvement, and you agree, you should then update the example and distribute the update to everyone on the team. This will make sure you are all "dancing to the same tune."

A couple of days or so after designers begin writing the blueprint, you should ask them to provide a few sample pages for your review. This will give you an opportunity to correct any problems before much time is invested.

Quality-Assure (QA) the Blueprint

After designers complete a first draft of the blueprint, you should review it and recommend revisions before it is distributed to SME and sponsor reviewers. Your quality assurance (QA) should be according to a set of predetermined criteria that designers are familiar with. (See Criteria for Internal QA of Blueprint.) This QA not only improves the quality of the blueprint, but helps you, as project manager, keep in touch with the details of the course. In this way, you can make more intelligent decisions and retain your credibility with SMEs and the sponsor.

At about the same time as you are performing QA, you should phone the SME and sponsor reviewers and remind them that they will be receiving the blueprint soon. You might also confirm the time and place where you will be meeting with them to receive their feedback.

Distribute to Reviewers

After the blueprint is completed, it is ready to distribute to reviewers. You might want to include a brief cover letter to help them focus on important issues and to clarify your deadline for receiving their feedback. (See the sample letter to reviewers.) It's also a good idea to phone reviewers to confirm that they have received the blueprint and to ask if they have any initial reactions. Since reviewers are usually among the busiest people in the organization, an extra phone call or two to check their progress can help them give your project a high priority. (Remember: the squeaky wheel gets the grease!)

The following tools can help you perform your internal QA of the blueprint and focus reviewers' attention on your requirements.

Criteria for Internal QA of Blueprint

Below are some typical criteria that you might want to apply when you perform your internal Quality Assurance (QA) review of the blueprint. By applying these criteria you can identify revisions for designers to make before submitting the blueprint for sponsor review.

☐ Evaluate objectives and their flow to see if: (1) flow and sequencing are sensible (2) there are no holes or gaps.

☐ Evaluate objectives one more time to assure that there is an appropriate mix of low level and high level objectives. (Are students asked to apply what they know, or are they simply asked to state facts and principles?)

☐ Evaluate the match between objectives and planned activities. Are students given opportunity to practice the objectives?

☐ Examine the summary of materials. Is it clear how many pieces of each media type will be created? Is it clear how these pieces will fit together?

☐ Examine the rationale for the design based on the results of task analysis and information gathering. *QA*

☐ Evaluate the content outline to assure it is accurate and contains the required level of detail.

☐ Review the descriptions of modules, chapters, etc. Make sure:

  – Each content statement matches (directly supports) its objective. There should be only necessary content; eliminate "nice-to-know" information.

  – Each statement of instructional strategy describes (1) how students will be presented with the content (2) what students will **do** to acquire or practice the skill described in the objective, and (3) what form of feedback students will get on their behavior

☐ Evaluate the summary of deliverables to determine conformity to budget and schedule. Identify places where deliverables might be cut, if necessary. *QA / QC*

☐ Consider the implementation requirements. Will the course meet the needs of those people who will be delivering it? Will the course be physically constructed so as to work well in the training environment? *QA*

Sample Cover Letter to Reviewers of the Blueprint

Below is a sample cover letter which is designed to be sent to reviewers along with their copy of the blueprint. Note how it focuses attention on key issues and helps direct his or her efforts.

Dear Reviewer:

Enclosed is the blueprint (design plans) for the _____ course. Information gathered from you earlier by our design team has been incorporated into this document. To help us create the best possible training, please do the following:

Write your questions and comments directly in the document as they occur to you. This will help speed up debriefing.

Answer these questions, in general:

- Is the instructional strategy sensible? Do you think it will work? If not, specifically why not?

- Does the course appear to be fun? If not, why not?

- Is the content accurate? Is anything out of date?

Your help is critical. If you don't have time to review the whole document, then please examine _____ *(whichever sections, pages, etc., depend on this reviewer's accuracy).*

Please don't give us vague or general feedback. We need to know exactly what is wrong and/or how to fix it.

If we don't hear from you by _____ *(deadline)* then we will assume that the document has been approved by you based on your area of responsibility. *(Needless to say, copies of the letter to each reviewer should be filed for later proof of their default approval, if necessary.)*

SMEs only: Provide your feedback directly to the sponsor. This way the sponsor can weigh it against other information from other reviewers and decide what to recommend to the design team.

Thanks for your help.

Obtain Feedback and Sign-off

After the sponsor and SMEs are finished reviewing your blueprint, you will need to carefully orchestrate their feedback. This isn't as simple as it sounds, especially if there are several reviewers. Here's why.

On most projects there is the possibility of disagreement among reviewers. Typically, SMEs have a greater knowledge of the content than does the sponsor. Sponsors are usually higher level managers who cannot stay on top of all the details. Yet sponsors are usually responsible for seeing that corporate philosophy and values are reflected in the training. So there may be disagreement between what an SME says is "true" and what your sponsor says is "true." Even worse, there may be disagreement between two SMEs about technical details.

Your design team should not try to sort out the disagreements among SMEs and the sponsor. To do so is to assume the responsibilities of the sponsor. Before you meet to obtain his or her feedback, the sponsor should have received the input from each SME and weighed conflicting opinions. Your design team can then be presented with a unified "party line" about specific changes in the training or the content.

In addition to the possibility of conflicting opinion on the sponsor's team, there is a chance that your design team will have some disagreements. For example, a designer may want to use a media treatment to which a production person objects. It is your responsibility, as project manager, to resolve these differences before you meet with the client to approve the blueprint.

The point is, you need a "chain of command" to help make these decisions efficiently. As we recommended in Chapter 3, major project decisions should be made jointly by the project manager and the sponsor. Figure 5-3 reiterates this recommended flow.

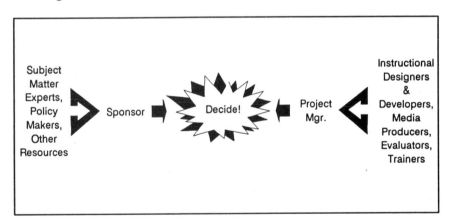

Figure 5-3: Project Decision Making

When the project manager and the sponsor have each obtained a unified set of recommendations from the people who report to them, you are ready to hold the sponsor feedback meeting. At the feedback meeting, you should "walk through" the blueprint one page at a time. Point to a page, then ask the sponsor what, specifically, must be changed on that page. Then move on to the next page, until the entire document is completely reviewed.

Finally, while it's important to plan and orchestrate this feedback, it is equally important to obtain closure on this step of the project so that you can go on to develop drafts. That's where a "sign-off" comes in. A secondary goal of the feedback meeting is to obtain your sponsor's approval of the blueprint in the form of a signed statement; that is, you need to get his or her "sign-off." This signed statement should acknowledge 1) that the sponsor approves the blueprint and, 2) that the sponsor understands that subsequent changes in structure or content could lead to a schedule delay and/or increased costs. (For a sample sign-off form, see Chapter 3, How to Organize the Project).

After you have obtained this approval, you are ready to begin creating draft instructional materials.

Conclusion

This chapter has described how to manage Step 4 of the project management model: Develop the Blueprint. First, it defined a blueprint and reviewed its importance in creating effective instructional materials. Next, it described the role of the project manager in developing the blueprint, conducting internal quality assurance, distributing to reviewers, and obtaining sponsor feedback and sign-off.

In the next chapter we will examine Step 5 of the ID project management process, Create Draft Materials.

Chapter 6

How to Create Draft Materials

So far in this book we have presented a typical ID project management model, an overview of the project manager's job in implementing the model, and some techniques for completing project planning tasks during Step 1: Determine Project Scope and Step 2: Organize the Project. In the last two chapters, we reviewed some techniques for managing Step 3: Gather Information and Step 4: Develop the Blueprint.

This chapter describes how to manage Step 5: Create Draft Materials.

What Are Draft Materials?

Recall that the output of the preceding step of the development process was the blueprint (sometimes called "design document," "design specifications," or "design plans"). This blueprint includes information on audience, course flow, performance objectives, instructional strategy, media and materials, and bulletted listings of content. In short, the blueprint represents the skeleton or "bare bones" of the course.

Draft materials "flesh out" the skeleton of the blueprint. That is, when you create draft materials you build on the blueprint to take the course to the next level of completion. So draft versions of course materials include the following elements that are **not** found in blueprints:

- Introductions

- Transitions

- Activities, exercises, practice sessions

- Job aids

- Text and rough draft graphic treatment of content

- Scripts for audio-visual media

- Flowcharts and storyboards for computer-based training

The physical format of these materials varies from organization to organization depending on the resources available. They may be created by typewriters, inexpensive dot-matrix printers, or laser printers. They may include hand-sketched graphics or computer-generated artwork.

However, all draft materials have three things in common:

- They are created by quick and easy production techniques.

- They may be revised quickly and easily.

- They contain the same level of detail as the finished course.

Why Bother Creating Draft Materials?

Sponsors sometimes ask, "Why bother creating draft materials? Why not simply go ahead and produce the finished materials so we can get the course up and running sooner?" Here's why you need to create draft materials.

One of the main goals of project management is to prevent wasted time and effort while ensuring a quality finished product. In that spirit, our last chapter recommended creating a blueprint which allows sponsors, SMEs, and other members of the design team to "tear apart" the course plans when they are in skeletal form. This way you minimize damage to completed materials, yet encourage thorough review of the course structure at a point when it is comparatively easy to revise.

In this same spirit, you should create draft materials to be reviewed by sponsors and SMEs and then tested with members of the target audience. These drafts may then be revised prior to production. It makes no sense to go to the trouble of carefully typesetting print materials, producing and editing audio-visual materials, and otherwise polishing the course when you have not assured that the content is correct and the materials "work" with members of the target audience. So the bottom line is that you create a draft version of the course to prevent having to revise materials that cost a lot of time and money to produce.

What Should Your Drafts Include?

Earlier we listed some things that are typically included in draft materials. Unfortunately, there can be no hard and fast rule for exactly what you should include in your particular set of drafts. This will differ from project to project. As a general rule, however, your **drafts should:**

- Include enough to allow thorough review by SMEs and the sponsor — (Give them all the content you intend to put in the finished course!)

- Include samples or prototypes with those features of page layout or other production that are essential to make the course "work"

- Include enough logistical polish to allow the course to be accurately tested with members of the target audience

- Exclude any features that are costly to produce or revise

For example, using the above guidelines, you would not attempt to produce "rough cut" video tapes for reviewers. These are too costly to revise. Instead, you would provide reviewers with detailed scripts and storyboards. On the other hand, if you were working on a computer-based course, you might need to go ahead and produce a couple of prototype lessons on disk, to allow reviewers to get the "feel" of the course. At the same time, you might provide the majority of the computer-based lessons for reviewers in written and sketched paper form. This way you could get their feedback and make revisions before committing hours to programming and linking lessons.

Your Role as Manager

If you have been following the recommended development process, the last activity that your design team completed was to develop the blueprint. In particular, you obtained your sponsor's approval of the blueprint in the form of a written sign-off. So now you and your design team are ready to create draft materials.

Below are the sub-steps you will need to perform. To complete these you will need to plan carefully, stimulate the right action at the right time, and intervene intelligently.

- Create draft materials according to blueprint specifications.

- Quality-assure (QA) the materials and revise if needed.

- Distribute the materials to reviewers.

- Obtain reviewer feedback and sponsor sign-off.

- Revise the materials in preparation for testing.

The chart on the next page summarizes this process. Now let's examine each sub-step.

Create Draft Materials

Before your design team begins to create draft materials, you should make certain that everyone is using the same format. You should locate or create a sample draft module or chapter showing any required page layouts, storyboard structures, and so on. If you don't share formats with designers before they begin, they will be forced to invent their own. Your sample should specify types of headings used, approaches for setting up exercises, use of headers and footers, and so on.

You should share these sample materials with the designers, making sure they understand how they work. If someone suggests an improvement, and you agree, you should then update the sample and distribute the update to everyone on the team. This will help assure that the formats of all draft materials will be consistent. A couple of days after designers begin writing the drafts, you should ask them to provide a few sample pages for your review. This will give you a chance to correct any format problems before they invest a lot of time.

If your course requires A-V media, then ask for a full media treatment before the scriptwriter jumps into writing scripts and storyboards. (You have probably already obtained a general media treatment as part of your blueprint. It doesn't hurt, however, to revise or confirm this treatment with scriptwriters before they begin writing draft scripts.)

Manager Role / Activity	Plan	Stimulate Action	Intervene
Create Draft Materials	Find or make examples of drafts	Share examples with designers; Set deadlines	Examine samples of each ID's drafts
Quality-Assure	Assemble QA criteria	Get drafts from each ID and QA	Provide feedback
Distribute to Reviewers	Prepare sponsor and SMEs	Send drafts and provide guidelines for review	Call and check progress
Obtain Feedback and Signoff	Set up meeting for feedback	Start meeting; Review drafts page-by-page	Keep team focused; Obtain signoff
Revise for Testing	Obtain annotated copy of drafts	Set deadlines for revision	Compare revisions to annotations

Figure 6-1: Manager Activities During Create Draft Materials

If you are building interactive or computer-based instruction, you will need to review and approve flowcharts or other organizational tools before designers start writing lessons.

Quality-Assure (QA)

After designers complete a first draft of their materials, you should review them and recommend revisions before they are distributed to SME and sponsor reviewers. This Quality Assurance (QA) should be according to a set of predetermined criteria that designers are familiar with. (See Suggested Guidelines for Internal QA of Drafts.) This QA not only improves the quality of the drafts, but helps you, as project manager, keep in touch with the details of the course. In this way, you can make more intelligent decisions and retain your credibility with SMEs and the sponsor.

There are several options for structuring the QA and review process:

Option 1: Ask designers to present you with one completed draft module or lesson at a time. This should provide plenty of time for a thorough evaluation of each.

If you choose this method, however, **do not** hold a feedback/review session with the designer after you finish each module. Save your comments until you have your feedback on the entire course. Here is our reasoning: Designing and writing new materials is a very different kind of task than getting feedback and revising materials. Most designers prefer to focus on one task or the other. To ask them to do both at the same time can cause frustration and schedule delays.

Option 2: Have the designer complete "chunks" of course components (i.e., all instructor notes, all role plays, all quizzes, etc.) and turn in each chunk as it is completed. As with Option 1, save your feedback on each until later.

Option 3: Do not ask the designer to give you any interim materials other than the preliminary samples. The advantage of this is that you may "go away" and concentrate on other chores while the designer is writing. The disadvantage is that, when the time comes, you must spend a large block of time (often one or two days) doing nothing but your internal review of materials.

At about the same time as you are performing the QA, you should phone the SME and sponsor reviewers and remind them that they will be receiving the drafts soon. This will help them set aside time for review. You might also confirm the time and place where you will be meeting with them to receive their feedback.

Distribute to Reviewers

After the drafts are completed, they are ready to distribute to reviewers. You should include a brief cover letter to help them focus on important issues and to clarify your deadline for receiving their feedback. (See the sample letter to reviewers.) It's also a good idea to phone reviewers to confirm that they have received the drafts and to ask for their preliminary reactions. Remember: Reviewers are usually among the busiest people in the organization. So an extra phone call or two can help to keep your project a high priority.

The next few pages provide some guidelines to help you complete your QA of draft materials and solicit feedback from reviewers.

Suggested Guidelines for Internal QA of Drafts

Follow these steps to complete your QA (quality assurance) of draft materials:

A. **Review (skim) the blueprint.** Refamiliarize yourself with the design and content of the course as approved by your sponsor and the SMEs.

B. **Make a broad brush review of draft materials** and determine:

☐ Is the overall flow and structure as promised in the blueprint?

☐ Is all the content promised by the blueprint present? Be prepared to explain and justify deviations to the sponsor, if necessary.

C. **Review the draft materials in detail** and determine:

☐ Is there a match between the objectives and the corresponding practice activity or test?

☐ Are there skills and concepts that are not covered but which should be covered?

☐ Are there enough examples? Will the examples make sense to the audience?

☐ Is there too much practice of a particular skill?

☐ Is the writing style appropriate for the medium?

☐ Are sentences short and to the point?

☐ Are transitions present and do they provide adequate "set up" for the information to follow?

☐ Does the language in scripts sound conversational where appropriate, or is it stilted?

☐ Does the author use enough advance organizers (overviews)?

☐ Are there reviews at the end of each section?

☐ Is the tone ever "preachy" or does the author talk down to the audience?

☐ Is humor used in a way that will not offend certain groups or "fall flat" with others?

☐ Are text pages and screens well designed?

☐ Are instructor notes clear and usable as references? (Did the author use easy-to-read phrases instead of fully scripting the text?)

☐ Are job aids clear and simple to follow?

☐ Are job aids tied in to the course via practice exercises?

☐ Are step-by-step exercises easy to follow?

☐ Do the materials meet the implementation requirements? (Are they usable in the "real world" training sites?)

☐ Are there more materials than we agreed to in the blueprint?

- If so, are the increases justifiable from an instructional perspective?

- If increased deliverables are justifiable, can they be supported by the budget and the schedule?

Other criteria, specific to this project:

☐ _____

☐ _____

☐ _____

☐ _____

☐ _____

☐ _____

☐ _____

☐ _____

☐ _____

☐ _____

Sample Cover Letter to Reviewers of the Draft Materials

Below is a sample cover letter which is designed to be sent to reviewers along with their copy of the blueprint. Note how it focuses attention on draft development issues and helps direct the reviewer's effort.

Dear Reviewer:

Enclosed, as promised, are the draft materials for the _____ course. Write questions and comments in the drafts as they occur to you. This will help speed up our debriefing session.

Please consider these questions:

- Has the instructional strategy as agreed to in the blueprint been fully realized? If not, specifically what has been missed?

- Is the content accurate? Is anything out of date?

- Does the course appear to be fun? If not, why not?

Your help is critical. If you don't have time to review the whole document, then please examine _____ *(whichever sections, pages, etc., depend on this reviewer's accuracy).*

If we don't hear from you by _____ *(deadline)* then we will assume that these draft materials have been approved by you based on your area of responsibility. *(Copies of the letter to each reviewer should be filed for later proof of their default approval, if necessary.)*

Please don't give us vague feedback! We need to hear exactly what is wrong and, if possible, how you would like to see the problem fixed.

SMEs only: Provide your feedback to _____ *(sponsor name).* S/he will forward it to the design team.

Thanks for your help.

Obtain Feedback and Sign-Off

After the sponsor and SMEs are finished reviewing your drafts, you will need to carefully orchestrate their feedback. This can be tricky, because of the possibility of disagreement among reviewers. (See Chapter 5 for a complete discussion of how to avoid snags in this feedback process.)

Your design team should not try to sort out the disagreements among SMEs and the sponsor. To do so is to assume the responsibilities of the sponsor. Before you meet to obtain his or her feedback, the sponsor should have received the input from each SME and should have weighed conflicting opinions. The sponsor can then present your design team with a unified "party line" about specific changes in the training or the content.

Caution: A sponsor might suggest that s/he not be held responsible for synthesizing the comments of SMEs, but that the SMEs, instead, should attend the review session with the design team and provide their comments in person. This latter method wastes time by making the group review longer than it need be and shifts responsibility for content accuracy to the design team, instead of with the sponsor, where it belongs. Your should insist that the sponsor come to the meeting with the synthesized comments of his or her reviewers.

At the feedback meeting, you should "walk through" the draft materials one page at a time. Ask the sponsor what must be changed on each page. Then move on to the next page, until all the drafts are completely reviewed.

Finally it is extremely important to obtain closure on this step of the project so that you can go on to prepare for the test of materials with members of the target audience. That's where a "sign-off" comes in.

Besides obtaining feedback, another goal of the feedback meeting is to obtain your sponsor's approval of the draft materials in the form of a signed statement; that is you need to get his or her "sign-off." This signed statement should acknowledge 1) that the sponsor approves the drafts and, 2) that the sponsor understands that subsequent changes in structure or content could lead to a schedule delay and/or increased costs. (For a sample sign-off form, see Chapter 3, Organize the Project).

After you have obtained this approval, you are ready to begin revising the draft instructional materials.

Revise for Testing

The approval of drafts by the sponsor (sign-off) is a two-way street. On the one hand it is the sponsor's assurance that s/he will not try to make capricious and arbitrary changes after you leave the feedback session. On the other hand this sign-off assumes that your project team will make the revisions as negotiated in the feedback session.

As project manager, you have an obligation to represent your sponsor's interests and assure that each change specified is actually executed by the design team. This means you must keep an annotated copy of the drafts and check each revision against this annotated copy.

By this point in the project, you and your entire design team may be getting a bit tired of the course. In addition, there may have been schedule delays that have meant that you are facing the next milestone, the testing of the materials, with not enough time for a thorough revision cycle. So there is a chance, at this point in the project, that revisions can slip through the cracks and never be executed.

The point is that you, as project manager, should stay alert and make sure all the revisions are actually made.

When the changes are complete, as agreed, then you are ready to move on to Step 6 of the development process, Test Draft Materials.

Conclusion

This chapter has described how to manage Step 5 of the project management model: Create Draft Materials. First, it defined draft materials and discussed why it is important to create drafts. Next, it outlined some key components of your draft materials and described the role of the project manager in managing the creation of drafts. In particular it described specific methods for internal quality assurance, distributing drafts to reviewers, obtaining sponsor feedback and sign-off, and revising prior to testing.

The next chapter in this book will provide some techniques for managing Step 6 of the ID project management process, Test Draft Materials.

Chapter 7

How to Test Draft Materials

So far in this book, we have presented a typical ID project management model, an overview of the project manager's job in implementing the model, and some techniques for completing project planning tasks during Step 1: Determine Project Scope and Step 2: Organize the Project. In the last three chapters, we reviewed some techniques for managing Step 3: Gather Information, Step 4: Develop the Blueprint, and Step 5: Create Draft Materials.

This chapter describes how to manage Step 6: Test Draft Materials.

Some Distinctions and a Definition

There are many terms that describe the activities discussed in this chapter. "Formative evaluation," "field test," "pilot test," and "alpha test" are just some of the labels that might apply. Admittedly, texts on instructional development often make important distinctions among these. For the most part, however, the job of the project manager remains much the same when planning and managing any of the activities to which these terms refer. Therefore, we will simply lump these all together under the term "test draft materials."

Recall that in the previous step of the development process we completed the draft materials. The physical format of draft materials varies from organization to organization. For example, some produce beautiful typeset materials, while others create materials with hand-drawn sketches and inexpensive dot-matrix printed pages. Yet whatever their physical format, **draft materials have at least three things in common:**

- They are produced quickly and easily.

- They may be revised quickly and easily.

- They contain the same level of detail as the finished course.

In short, draft materials are designed with the expectation that they will be revised — and it is the testing of draft materials which determines exactly how they will be revised.

With all this in mind, we offer this **definition:** *The phrase "test draft materials" means to conduct a trial run of the courseware to make sure that the materials work the way they were designed to work.* The physical environment, the instructor, the target audience, and the instructional materials should be as close to the "real thing" as possible, while keeping production costs (and presumably production values) to a minimum.

Why Bother Testing Draft Materials?

Sponsors sometimes ask, "Why bother testing draft materials? Why not simply go ahead and produce the finished materials so we can get the course up and running sooner?" Here's how you might answer:

The purpose of conducting a test is to get the reactions of students to the materials and events of the course. It is an opportunity to check how clear, as well as how effective, the materials are. What's more, it is an opportunity to check to see if people actually attain the objectives (acquire the proposed skills) when they take the course. Finally, testing materials before they are produced allows the design team to make final refinements to the course before spending the time and money to produce the master materials, distribute them, and train members of the target audience.

While the test does not provide validation, or absolute proof, that the materials will work when they are implemented in the field, it is an important step toward "reality checking" the materials. In short, the test of training materials is similar to the "beta test" of a new product; it's the time to identify some of the bugs before the finished product is released. Just as you wouldn't buy a car without a test drive, you wouldn't implement a course without a test of its effectiveness.

Your Role as Manager

According to our development process, the last activity that your design team completed was to create draft materials. Now you are ready to test these drafts. Here are the sub-steps you will need to perform:

- Obtain test subjects, members of the target audience, with whom you will conduct the test.

- Prepare for the test by assembling copies of the draft materials, setting up the test site, making course critiques, and so on.

- Conduct the test.

- Debrief with participants and observers.

- Determine revisions to the draft materials.

To complete these you will need to plan carefully, stimulate the right action at the right time, and intervene intelligently. The chart below summarizes.

Manager Role ↓ Activity ➡	Plan	Stimulate Action	Intervene
Obtain Test Subjects	Review audience assumptions; List requirements	Contact sponsor; Request attendees; Set deadlines	"Nag" as needed
Prepare for Test	Determine evaluation strategy; Review logistics	Assign responsibilities; Set deadlines	Check progress
Conduct Test	Prepare and review ground rules	Start session; Coordinate observers	Keep test moving; Check obervers' notes
Debrief	Review debriefing strategy	Conduct debriefing sessions	Keep discussions focused and relevant
Determine Revisions	Analyze data gathered	Meet with IDs and sponsor; Specify revisions	Negotiate; Obtain signoff

Figure 7-1: Manager Activities During Test Draft Materials

Obtain Test Subjects

A good test session should be populated somewhat like Noah's ark — it should include at least two of every kind. So if your identified target audience consists of experienced repair people, you should have at least two experienced repair people at the test. If your audience also includes new hires, then you should include at least two new hires. We prefer to hold the total number of test subjects to between 8 and 12 people for testing most types of courseware. A group this size typically provides plenty of variation in its reactions, yet is not so large that the test becomes unmanageable.

Finding test participants isn't always easy. It is sometimes tough for busy members of the target audience to become enthusiastic participants in your test. In fact, it is sometimes the case that you find yourself frantically searching for test participants at the last minute. What this can mean is that anybody who can participate is cheerfully accepted. While this might meet your need to complete the test, it certainly doesn't contribute much to course quality. After all, how valuable are their opinions if these test subjects are not truly representative of your actual target audience?

It's much better to be proactive. You should carefully review the assumptions that have been made about the audience and then make a list of the ideal test participants. When you have listed your requirements, you'll be able to contact your sponsor and request that he or she provide you with the people you need. You may have to set a deadline with the sponsor for providing these people. Then, when the deadline approaches, some friendly reminders (a little nagging, maybe?) might be in order.

The following worksheet might help.

Guidelines for Obtaining Test Subjects

Perform these steps to obtain subjects for your test of draft materials:

Step 1: Review the assumptions regarding the target audience as presented in the course blueprint or analysis documents.

Step 2: List the broad job titles that are eligible for the training. (For example, customer service reps, sales reps, repair technicians, etc.).

Job Title A: _____

Job Title B: _____

Job Title C: _____

Step 3: Within each job title you listed in Step 2, name the subcategories of people you want to attend the test. For example, of all the sales reps who should attend, you want two who are high achievers, two who are experienced but average performers, two new hires, and so on. (Ignore the "Names" column for now.)

Job Title A: _____   **Names:**

Type 1: _____   a. _____

b._____

Type 2: _____   a. _____

b._____

Type 3: _____   a. _____

b._____

Job Title B: _____   **Names:**

Type 1: _____   a. _____

b._____

Type 2: _____   a. _____

b._____

Type 3: _____   a. _____

b._____

Job Title C: _____   **Names:**

Type 1: _____   a. _____

                                     b._____

Type 2: _____   a. _____

                                     b._____

Type 3: _____   a. _____

                                     b. _____

Step 4:   Review and revise the list above. Try to limit the list to between 8 and 12 individuals.

Step 5:   Ask the sponsor to come up with names of people who are of the type you need. Write each of their names beside the appropriate "type" in the "Names" column.

Step 6:   Ask the sponsor to contact these people or their supervisors (depending upon proper protocol) and get a commitment for their attendance on the dates scheduled.

Benefits (selling points) your sponsor can cite for getting them to attend include:

- They will be one of the first in their office to learn about the new product or process.

- They will be able to get to know other "early adopters" (leaders) who have been chosen to evaluate the course.

- They will be able to help shape the course, thus contributing to the organization's overall success with the product or process.

Prepare for the Test

Whether you prepare the test yourself or have members of your design team prepare the test, there is much to be done to make sure everything goes smoothly.

In the first place, you must determine what type of evaluation methodology you will use. Typically, the design team gathers information from several sources. These sources include:

- Periodic debriefing sessions with participants, in which they provide you with questions, reactions, and suggestions for revision

- Notes from observers who use structured observation forms to capture reactions and interactions of participants

- Written course critiques, completed by participants after each segment of the course

This list is by no means exhaustive. There are entire texts written on evaluation techniques, so we will not presume in this brief space to provide detailed guidance on the subject. The point is, however, that the manager must work with the design team to plan some sort of evaluation strategy and then see to it that the tools (questionnaires, checklists, etc.) for executing these strategies are created. This assumes that the manager must assign the task of building these tools to someone on the design team, set deadlines, and see to it that the tools are completed.

In addition, the manager and the design team should review the "course choreography" (who does what, with what, when) and make sure that all the logistical details are accounted for. Materials, equipment, refreshments, and other details must be carefully planned.

The following checklist can help you remember what you need to do.

Checklist: Test Preparation Chores

Use this checklist to help complete your test preparations.

☐ Review your evaluation strategy and list the kinds of tools you will need.

  ☐ Participant debriefing forms for use by interviewers

  ☐ Observation checklists, rating forms, and instructions for observers on how to use them

  ☐ Module and course critique forms for use by participants

  ☐ Overall evaluation strategy description

☐ Assign someone the responsibility to build each of the tools identified above.

☐ Notify participants in writing of date, time, location, housing arrangements, etc. Emphasize in the letter that it is the course that will be evaluated, not the participants. Provide them with an honest estimate of the time they will likely have to spend.

☐ Make sure all the revisions have been made to the drafts, as agreed to in the draft review with the sponsor.

☐ Make sure drafts are as clean as possible. If there is time and the content is relatively stable, you might consider having them copy edited before final typing.

☐ If rough art work has been used for draft review, make certain that polished, clean versions are created for the test. (Clean, though not necessarily professionally-produced, art work is required.)

☐ Make sure audio visual scripts are clean and easy to read. If possible, provide storyboards to help bring video scripts to life.

Caution: Do *not* create "rough cut" versions of video or audio productions for the test. This is usually more trouble and expense than it is worth. (Rough cuts can be more confusing to test participants than simply reading a messy script.)

☐ Determine the test location and check it for adequacy (lighting, electrical outlets, ventilation, room for special activities, special arrangements of furniture, etc.).

Note: For the most accurate test of the training, choose a location which will be as close to the "real world" implementation environment as possible.

☐ Set up and test any special equipment required for hands-on activities or demonstrations.

☐ Make sure you have enough copies of support documentation for each student, if needed (job aids, tech manuals, etc.).

☐ Rehearse with the trainer, if appropriate.

   ☐ "Walk through" the course with the instructor, page by page, to provide an overview of the "choreography."

   ☐ Allow the instructor a couple of days to prepare for the rehearsal independently.

   ☐ Assemble all the materials and equipment needed for the course and set up the room.

   ☐ Conduct the rehearsal. If time is limited, focus the instructor's effort on the following:

   – All lectures (including presentation support media such as overhead transparencies)

   – All introductions to media presentations

   – All introductions to exercises, role plays, or other special activities

   – Procedures for questioning, observing, or providing feedback to students

☐ Plan healthful snacks and meals. Do not give people sugar-based products that will alter their alertness or mood. Fruit, nuts, or vegetables are good snack choices. Avoid heavy, high-carbohydrate lunches.

☐ Review all evaluation tools that have been created by your designers and make sure interviewers and reviewers know how to use them.

☐ On the day of the test (before participants get there) arrange equipment and materials. Be sure you know where everything is. Have pencils, name cards, writing pads, etc.

Note: Your completed course will likely have in it a list of all the materials, equipment, and so on that are required to conduct the course. You should modify this list accordingly as you prepare the test and assemble the materials which you are "really" going to use.

Conduct the Test

After you have obtained the names of people who will attend your pilot and have made your preparations, you are ready to run the test.

At the beginning of the test, you need to introduce yourself and review your ground rules with participants. Later, during the test, you need to make sure that IDs and observers are getting the kind of information they need without being obtrusive. And finally, you need to make sure the training moves along, without getting bogged down in irrelevancies.

(See the guidelines beginning on the next page.)

Debrief

The purpose of a debriefing session is to gather oral feedback from test participants. Compared to written feedback, oral feedback can more easily reveal participants' strong feelings, while allowing your design team the chance to probe by asking additional questions. This can shed light on hard-to-articulate issues.

If your course is relatively short (1/2 day or so) you may get by with a single debriefing session. For longer courses, you will probably want to debrief after each module or subsection. In this case, a summary or wrap-up debriefing session may also be appropriate.

We assume that a designer or an evaluation professional will write the debriefing questions. If you, as project manager, must construct your own questions and you have no formal training in this type of evaluation, you should consult a good text on instructional design or evaluation.

When planning the debriefing session, review the designer's or evaluator's strategy to make sure it seems complete and all questions are appropriate. During the debriefing session, make sure that all comments are captured and that discussions stay focused and relevant.

(See the debriefing guidelines that follow.)

Guidelines for Conducting the Test

Use these guidelines to help conduct an effective test of draft materials.

Getting Started

At the beginning of the test session, you should:

☐ Start on time. Don't reinforce the behavior of arriving late by waiting for slow pokes. (Have an assistant quietly bring late arrivers up-to-date at the side or back of the classroom.)

☐ Introduce yourself and all other observers. State what your roles will be during the test, but downplay your ranks in the organization in order to prevent test subjects from "performing" for your benefit.

☐ Assure participants that their ideas and suggestions are needed and valuable. Explain that ideas which were clear to the writers of the course may not be clear to them — it is just such problems with the course that you want to find.

☐ Emphasize that it is the course materials which are being tested, not the participants.

☐ Urge participants to carefully perform all exercises as instructed and make notes of any problems or confusion they experience. Urge them to write their notes on the materials, rather than rely on memory for their debriefing sessions later.

☐ Explain that you will be meeting with the participants and debriefing later. You will collect their comments at that time.

☐ Suggest that participants do not waste valuable test time marking typographical errors or grammatical mistakes. Explain that these will be caught by the copy editor later.

While the Test Is Under Way:

After the test has begun, observe these guidelines:

☐ **If self-study materials are being tested**, make sure people may move through the materials at their own pace. You might, however, set general targets for completion time. Plan to release people who finish before others (though don't announce this as policy).

☐ *Caution your designers and observers:* During the test session you will find people get "stuck" or confused. It is hard to watch people struggle when you know the answer or when you know how to perform the task. In any case, when you see a student having a problem with a given quiz or task or even having difficulty understanding a presentation, you should not attempt to help. Instead, **when someone is confused, follow these steps:**

  ☐ Discretely **notify the instructor** to see if the instructor might be able to help the student. If there is no instructor, go on to the next step.

  ☐ **Find out exactly what is confusing the student.** Was it something s/he read? Was it something the instructor said? Was it a media presentation?

  ☐ **Write down, in detail, the exact problem** and where and when in the course materials it occurred. You will need to refer to this information in your debriefing session later.

  ☐ **Now (at last!) you can help** the student. But remember to document exactly what information you had to provide the student in order to end the student's confusion.

☐ **Do not allow yourself or the designer to butt into the instructor's presentation.** This could cause a loss of credibility for the instructor and, ultimately, the entire design team. A better method would be to call a brief "time out" and discuss the problem with the instructor outside the range of student hearing.

☐ **Make sure observations take place unobtrusively** and exactly as planned.

☐ **Make sure course critiques and other debriefing tools are used** exactly as planned.

☐ **Keep things moving and on time.** One result of the test session is that you can document how long each instructional activity takes to perform. If you let people drift into irrelevant discussions, you might not get an accurate account of the time required.

☐ *(Optional)* **Make sure participants return their course materials** before they leave. Assure them that they will get the new, improved version of the course materials as soon as they are revised. In this way you can prevent dissemination of your course materials before they are revised and completely accurate

Test Debriefing Guidelines

Here are some general guidelines for conducting debriefing sessions with the people who attended the test session.

☐ Make sure you **schedule enough time** during the test to conduct the debriefings.

☐ **Give participants time to "pull together" their notes** before the session begins. (Five or ten minutes should be plenty of time.)

☐ **Consider audio taping the participants' comments.** This can help you keep up with the discussion more easily than if you are forced to take notes and ask questions at the same time.

☐ **Consider using an outside evaluator** — someone not on the design team — to conduct the debriefing sessions. This neutral party may be able to avoid some of the traps described below.

☐ **Remind designers** before the debriefing that **they must not defend the course or rationalize;** rather they should simply gather responses to the debriefing questions. (Remember, if participants must listen to rationalizations in response to each of their complaints, they will probably limit their complaints — and skew your test results.)

☐ Interrupt or tactfully stop anyone on the design team who defends or attempts to rationalize design decisions. Steer the discussion back towards getting only the debriefing questions answered.

☐ **Make sure everyone has a chance to provide opinions.** If someone tries to dominate the discussion, ask other participants, by name, how they feel about the point that the dominating person is making.

☐ **Don't "lead the witness."** That is, make sure designers don't use non-verbal cues (nods, smiles, sniffs of disapproval) or verbal paraphrasing ("So you say the hands-on activity was very stimulating?") to elicit particular kinds of responses. (While these examples may sound silly, they are all too real. It is only human nature to actively seek approval from people when you have spent weeks or months developing a course for them.)

☐ If they aren't already on your list, **consider asking these questions** at the end of the session:

  ☐ Do you have any opinions that you haven't expressed?

  ☐ If you could wave a magic wand and make two improvements in the course, what would they be?

Determine Revisions

When the dust settles and the participants have gone home, you and your design team will have accumulated a lot of information about what needs improving in the course. You will have notes from debriefing sessions, notes from observers, completed participant critique sheets, and the participants' annotated course materials.

Your design team's next chores will be to analyze all of this data, meet with the sponsor and recommend revisions, and obtain the sponsor's approval.

The following guidelines can be used to help you complete these chores.

How to Determine Revisions

In order to determine required revisions after completing your test session, follow these steps:

Step 1: Ask your designers to **review the notes, critiques, and other documentation from the test** and create a summary of course problems and recommended solutions. (Allow no more than a day or so for this activity.)

Step 2: **Review the problems and recommendations with the design team** and provide input as appropriate.

Step 3: Meet with your design team, the sponsor, and (if appropriate) the trainer and **"walk through" the entire course page by page.** As you come to a portion of the course which someone believes should be revised, do this:

☐ Discuss the data which supports the revision.

☐ Discuss the pros and cons of the revision. (Remember budget and schedule impact.)

☐ Agree to the exact wording and form of the revision.

☐ Determine if another test would be required after revisions are made. (Avoid this, unless you have scheduled it or you have all decided that the course must undergo substantial revision.)

☐ Determine deadlines for SMEs to resolve any questionable content details. (These are based on production dates.)

Step 4: **Ask for the sponsor's approval in the form of a written sign-off** which states his or her acknowledgment that:

☐ The tested materials have been approved, with changes as noted in the master copy.

☐ The design team may use the annotated masters of the tested materials as the basis for revisions and creating production masters.

☐ Any further changes in content or structure (beyond those identified at present) will likely result in increased costs and/or schedule delays.

Conclusion

This chapter has described how to manage Step 6 of the project management model: Test Draft Materials. First, it defined the phrase "test draft materials" and provided a rationale for conducting the test. Next, it described how to obtain test subjects and prepare for the test session. In addition, it suggested some ground rules and guidelines for conducting the test and debriefing the participants. Finally, it described how to get closure on the required revisions before the materials move into production.

The next chapter in this book will describe some techniques for managing Step 7 of the ID project management process, Produce Master Materials.

Chapter 8

How to Produce Master Materials

So far in this book, we have presented a typical ID project management model, an overview of the project manager's job in implementing the model, and some techniques for completing project planning tasks during Step 1: Determine Project Scope and Step 2: Organize the Project. In subsequent chapters, we reviewed some techniques for managing Step 3: Gather Information, Step 4: Develop the Blueprint, Step 5: Create Draft Materials, and Step 6: Test Draft Materials.

This chapter describes how to manage Step 7: Produce Master Materials.

Where Production Fits In

Instructional development is often characterized as an "iterative" process; that is, throughout the project the design team creates, modifies, then revises the instructional materials. First, the Blueprint is created, reviewed by SMEs and sponsor, and the instructional strategy is modified as needed. Next, the drafts are created, reviewed by SMEs and sponsor, and modified in preparation for testing. Finally, after testing, the drafts are revised in preparation for production.

Thus, by the time production begins, the materials should have undergone all substantive revisions. In other words, the materials should be ready to "freeze" into the form of the highest quality masters that your budget will allow. These will, in turn, be reproduced and distributed when training is implemented.

In some organizations, production and reproduction happen almost at the same time. For example, print materials could be desktop published, resulting in laser-printed copies that are nearly equivalent to typeset master materials. In this way the boundary between production and reproduction can be blurred. To help keep the issues in focus, however, we will assume that production and reproduction are separate tasks.

With this in mind, here's a definition: *The phrase "produce master materials" means to create one high-quality set of instructional materials from which reproductions may be made.* Physically, master materials may take the form of print, audio or video tape, computer disk, or any other medium. But whatever the medium, the master materials should be of the highest possible quality in order that they can be used to generate high-quality reproductions.

Instructional Integrity Versus Production Values

Let's assume that up to this point in the project instructional designers have developed draft materials which:

- reflect the needs of the training audience,

- accurately describe the product or process that is the topic of the course, and

- assure that the appropriate tasks are practiced by the audience.

In short, the designers have been careful that the materials have instructional integrity. Now it's time to "hand-over" the materials to production people.

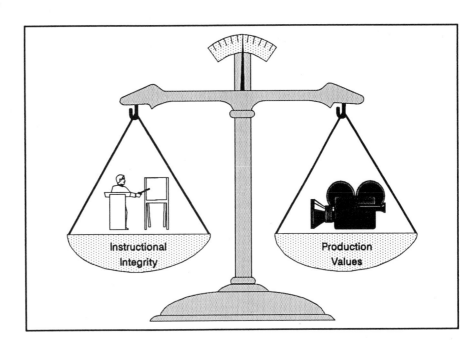

Figure 8-1: Finding the Balance During Production

Most production people are highly skilled professionals, motivated to create the best quality masters. Yet because they often join the design team relatively late in the project's evolution, they do not always "buy into" the decisions that went into the design of the training. What's more, some producers assign a greater value to beauty than they do to instructional integrity. After all, they are usually paid for their ability to attain high production values and not for their instructional design skills.

So in order to maintain the instructional integrity of the course, the design team must assert editorial control over the materials as they are produced. As leader of the design team, the project manager must make sure that the materials reflect the design specifications and subsequent decisions made by the team and the sponsor. (This role may be delegated to a designer, but for now, let's assume that the manager will be responsible.) The goal, then, is to achieve a balance between instructional integrity and production values.

Your Role as Manager

To maintain this balance and assure that quality master materials are produced the project manager should perform these sub-steps:

- Orient producers to the project.
- Establish the production method and schedule.
- Review samples of materials as they are available.
- Attend production sessions, when appropriate.
- Obtain sponsor approval of the master materials.

To complete these you will need to plan carefully, stimulate the right action at the right time, and intervene intelligently.

The following chart summarizes the process.

Activity / Manager Role	Plan	Stimulate Action	Intervene
Orient Producers	Prepare overview; Assemble latest drafts	Meet with producers; Show how pieces fit together	"Sell" design strategy; Discuss producer concerns
Establish Production Method/Schedule	List requirements of production design and schedule	Agree on production design/schedule with producers	Defend instructional integrity and sponsor's deadlines
Review Samples	Set deadlines for getting samples of each medium	Review and approve samples; Involve sponsors	Note deviations from the design; Specify revisions
Attend Production Sessions	Assemble and review draft materials and scripts	Attend production; Compare planned to actual	Note deviations from plan; Specify revisions
Obtain Sponsor Approval	Set up meeting to review masters; Assemble masters	Review masters with sponsor; Specify revisions	Keep sponsor focused; Get signoff

Figure 8-2: Manager Activities, Produce Master Materials

For the sake of clarity, this book treats each of these activities as if it happens solely within Step 7: Produce Master Materials. However, you might want to orient producers to the project, establish the production method and schedule, and start to review samples as early as Step 4: Develop the Blueprint. In general, the earlier that producers are involved, the better.

Now let's examine each sub-step.

Orient Producers

In Chapter 3: How to Organize the Project, it was recommended that you assign one production coordinator for each type of media that will be produced. For example, you might have a print production coordinator to work with the copy editor, layout people, graphics artist, and typesetters. In addition, you might have an audio-visual production coordinator to work with the scriptwriter, director, post production people, and so on. This can simplify your job by reducing the number of people whom you must directly coordinate. In addition, by having a seasoned production specialist perform the initial quality assurance of the media, you are likely to achieve better quality.

In any case, whether you decide to use production coordinators or work directly with the production people yourself, you will need to begin production by orienting the producers. This means that you must meet with them and show them how the pieces fit together and how the design strategy works. The better informed producers are about your instructional intent, the more they will be able to help you achieve that intent through their productions. Conversely, if they remain uninformed about the instructional design of the materials, they are likely to make all their decisions on the basis of production values alone. You could get materials which are "pretty" but not instructionally effective.

Establish Production Method and Schedule

After producers have been oriented to the required courseware, you will need to negotiate specific production methods or production designs. For example, will print materials be laser-printed or produced on a printing press? Or will videos be shot using actors or ordinary employees of your organization? What will be the overall "look and feel" of the materials when they are assembled into the finished package? These are the kinds of questions that must be discussed before production can begin. As project manager, your role in these discussions will be to assure that instructional integrity is maintained along with high production values. If possible, the sponsor should be involved in these decisions.

After you have decided on the production methods, you will need to develop a detailed production schedule. It is assumed the overall project schedule that you have been using to this point had broad time frames set aside for production. However, now that the drafts have been tested and revised and you have discussed various production methods, it's time to negotiate a detailed production schedule. Your role as project manager is to present your firm deadline requirements and then help producers figure out how to meet them.

Sometimes it's possible to hold a single orientation meeting in which you present producers with your requirements and then negotiate production methods and schedule. On the other hand, it may take a couple of sessions to work through all the issues.

The following are some guidelines for orienting producers and helping establish production methods and schedules.

Guidelines for the Production Orientation Meeting

Use these guidelines to plan an orientation meeting with producers.

Before you start the meeting:

☐ Obtain any production guidelines or standards which your organization imposes on training media.

For example, all print media must use 12 point, Times Roman typeface. Or all managers portrayed in videos must be dressed in formal business attire. (Such standards are especially important if you're using vendors who haven't worked with you before.)

☐ Assemble samples of produced materials (other courseware) that are similar to what you or your sponsor have in mind.

☐ Assemble copies of all draft materials.

☐ Assemble your schedule requirements (deadlines) for having materials ready for reproduction and distribution.

☐ Prepare an overview presentation that describes the "big picture" of the course you are creating.

At the meeting:

☐ Describe how the pieces fit together and what trainees will be doing when using them. (Knowing the context in which materials will be used can help producers tap their own creativity and produce more effective solutions.)

☐ Get excited about the design strategy and let your enthusiasm show. "Sell" it, if necessary.

☐ Show the samples of what you want and relate them to the draft materials produced so far and your organization's production guidelines.

☐ Describe which production decisions are firm (sponsor requirements that aren't negotiable) and which are open for suggestion.

☐ Present your schedule requirements and any firm deadlines.

☐ Discuss questions and handle producers' concerns.

☐ Get agreement on production methods and a detailed production schedule. [See Sample Production Checkpoints.]

After the meeting:

☐ Document the agreements in writing in a project status report. (See Chapter 3: How to Organize the Project for an example.)

☐ Send copies of the status report to all project players, including the sponsor.

☐ Make sure everyone on the project team gets a copy of the negotiated production schedule.

Typical Production Checkpoints

Below are some typical production checkpoints that can serve as deadlines during production. Assign specific dates to each.

Print Production

Date:	Checkpoint:
_____	Final drafts completed and provided to copy editor
_____	Copy-edited materials to ID and sponsor for review and approval
_____	Sample page layouts to ID and sponsor for review and approval
_____	Completed print masters to ID and sponsor for review and approval
_____	Print masters ready for final review/approval by sponsor
_____	Final, revised masters ready for reproduction

Audio-Visual Production

Date:	Checkpoint
_____	All necessary demo equipment, facilities, and people provided by sponsor
_____	Sets, cast, music, other aesthetic decisions approved by sponsor
_____	Rehearsal (with sponsor and ID observing)
_____	Shooting and recording sessions (with sponsor and ID observing)
_____	"Rough cut" or unedited media reviewed by sponsor and ID
_____	Sound mixing or visual editing sessions (with sponsor and ID observing)
_____	Masters ready for final review/approval by sponsor
_____	Final, revised masters ready for reproduction

> **NOTE:** Simulations, CAI, and other media productions will require that different check points be used. Modify the list above accordingly. No matter what you are producing, however, keep in mind these **two guidelines:** (1)Always obtain samples for review and approval before full-blown production efforts begin. (2)Make sure that you or your ID and your sponsor are present at all expensive, people-intensive production events.

Review Samples

Producing master materials is typically time-consuming and expensive. That's why it's important to check samples of the producers' output before they are too far along in the production cycle. In this way you can be sure that time and money aren't wasted on inappropriate production techniques.

Specifically, you should set deadlines for getting samples of all the different types of deliverables that will be produced. For example, your print production coordinator should provide you with a sample workbook page, a sample instructor page, a sample job aid, and samples of other types of print materials. Your A-V producer can provide you with sketches of sets, detailed treatment plans, audition tapes from potential cast members, and samples of tapes that are similar in treatment to the one you will be producing for your course.

When you obtain each set of samples, you should first review them with the course designer, making certain that they will meet your instructional requirements. When you and your designer have approved the samples, ask the sponsor to look at them and note any required revisions. After everyone on the design team approves the samples, the producers can continue their work secure in the knowledge that their production techniques have the whole team's blessing.

Attend Production Sessions

For most audio-visual productions, the efforts of many highly-paid people will be concentrated into a few critical days of shooting, recording, and editing. It is possible to consume a large percentage of the entire project budget in these few media production days. As project manager, you must make sure you get your money's worth. That's why you and your sponsor should attend these important sessions.

To prepare for the sessions, you should assemble and review the latest versions of the scripts and other draft materials (such as case study questions or job aids) which tie to the scripts. This will help you stay on top of things when you get to the production location. In fact, you may be the only one at the production who is paying attention to the big picture of how the various media fit together to make a course.

During the production, you can compare the scripted (planned) production with the actual production as it unfolds. Because you are there on the scene, you can correct technical errors as soon as they occur, while the set is up and the actors are together. This can prevent costly days of redressing sets, reshooting, or rerecording.

It is strongly recommended that the sponsor, major SMEs, and anyone else who is empowered to accept or reject the finished materials, attend the production with you. In this way, they not only get to share the excitement of the production, but they will get insight into the inevitable deviations from the script that must be made during production. In addition, the sponsor and SME can contribute much to the quality of the finished production as they note mispronunciations of technical terms, artificial mannerisms portrayed by actors, costumes that aren't quite right, and other problems that you or the design team might miss.

For detailed guidelines describing what to look for when evaluating print and audio-visual productions, see the checklists beginning on the next page.

Obtain Sponsor Approval

The final task in producing the master materials is to have your sponsor review and approve them. You or your instructional designer should review the materials yourself before presenting them for the sponsor's final review. The checklist on the next page includes some generic criteria for evaluating print and audio-visual masters. You should add your own specific review criteria for each course you are producing.

When you or your designer have completed your review of the masters, you are ready to assemble all the pieces and meet with the sponsor. At that meeting, you should "walk through," page-by-page, the print masters and review, when appropriate, any audio-visual or other media that fit into the course design.

Keep this in mind as you conduct this review: the sponsor has already approved all the draft materials and scripts when he or she signed off on the drafts and the results of the test session. Therefore, the purpose of this review is to approve the results of production only. It is not appropriate for the sponsor to rethink content or redesign the course at this point. For example, it would be appropriate for the sponsor to reject the placement of a graphic on a particular page, but it would not be appropriate for the sponsor to try to rewrite an entire introductory module of the course. The time for rewrites has passed. As project manager, it's your job to keep the sponsor's review focused on the production issues only.

When you and the sponsor have examined all the materials, you should conclude the meeting by asking for written approval (a sign-off) to move on to Step 8: Reproduce.

Print Production Evaluation Checklist

When checking print masters, keep in mind the following:

☐ Check to see that the meaning hasn't been distorted by the correction of grammar, punctuation, or spelling during copy-editing.

☐ Check to see that necessary technical terms are not "corrected" by the copy editor. (For example, "DOS" is an operating system, not a misspelled term.)

☐ Make sure you agree with specified page breaks.

☐ Check to see if the layout of sample "boards" or masters is exactly as you want it. In particular:

 – Look for plenty of white space in the text.

 – Make sure headlines and call outs are used effectively.

 – Make sure job aids appear easy to use, not cluttered.

 – Make sure that the instructional message is supported by, not upstaged by, the page design.

☐ Check completed masters against the copy-edited final drafts to assure that everything was properly transformed into the finished product.

☐ Make sure artwork is technically accurate; note especially the accuracy of labels and call outs.

☐ Other:

☐ Other:

Audio-Visual Production Evaluation Checklist

CAUTION: You should try to apply these evaluation criteria at the time you attend the production session. If you wait until masters are completely produced, it will be too late to make changes without reshooting or rerecording.

Video Productions

☐ Make sure the production visualization matches the scripts, storyboards, and other approved treatments.

☐ Make sure that the actors chosen to portray your characters truly reflect the role. Excessive beauty, bizarre appearance, unusual vocalizations, or other striking characteristics should be present in the chosen actor only if they support the instructional intent.

☐ If actors are to serve as role models, make sure they will exhibit the appropriate dress and demeanor.

☐ Make sure the set supports the purpose of the instruction. It should not call attention to itself unnecessarily.

☐ Make sure all equipment, objects, or backgrounds that are clearly visible to the audience are accurately depicted. (For example, have the SME check to see that technical equipment appears to be used realistically by the actors.)

☐ Look at the screen. Is the proper emphasis being given to technical equipment or other objects? Do you see the right objects on screen at the right time?

Audio Productions or Sound Track on Videos

☐ Make certain that all words written and approved in the script are spoken by the actors.

☐ Make sure that actors pronounce technical terms and phrases accurately and with the proper emphasis.

☐ If the director decides to leave dialogue out or change a line, be certain the sponsor approves. (If the sponsor isn't at the recording session, you will have to approve the change yourself. Be sure to document the change and be prepared to explain your reason for approving it.)

☐ Ask producers to play the finished audio tapes and audio portions of video tapes through a small, inexpensive speaker (similar to that which will be used by students). Does the sound have the same impact as in the studio, on expensive studio monitors? Will it need to be remixed to compensate for these "real world" conditions?

Overall Audio and Visual

☐ Is the pacing appropriate?

☐ Is the ratio of music to voice or the final editing mix of other sound effects right? Trust your judgment.

☐ Examine accuracy. Is the message still technically correct?

☐ Consider impact. Is the message powerfully expressed?

Conclusion

This chapter has described how to manage Step 7 of the project management model: Produce Master Materials. In particular, it described how the project manager might maintain a balance between production values and instructional integrity. In addition, it presented some techniques to help you orient producers to your instructional requirements and manage their efforts to achieve quality instructional media. Finally, it provided some guidelines for managing sponsor and SME participation in the production effort.

The next chapter will describe some techniques for managing the next two steps of the project management process, Step 8: Reproduce and Step 9: Distribute.

Chapter 9

How to Manage Reproduction and Distribution

The first chapter presented a typical ID project management model and an overview of the project manager's job in implementing the model. The next two chapters provided information on Phase I of the model, Project Planning, including techniques for completing Step 1: Determine Project Scope and Step 2: Organize the Project. The next five chapters presented information on Phase II of the model, Instructional Development. In particular, these chapters reviewed some techniques for managing Step 3: Gather Information, Step 4: Develop the Blueprint, Step 5: Create Draft Materials, Step 6: Test Draft Materials, and Step 7: Produce Master Materials.

(To review the model, refer to Figure 9-1: An ID Project Management Model, on the next page.)

In this chapter, our focus will shift to Phase III: Follow Up. In particular, we will examine some techniques for managing Step 8: Reproduce and Step 9: Distribute. While these are listed as separate steps in the model, they will be discussed together here, since many of the activities to be performed, as well as the people who must perform them, often overlap.

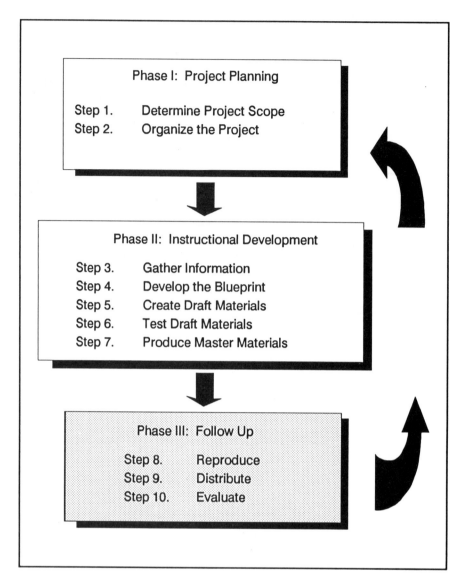

Figure 9-1: Typical Project Management Model

About Reproduction and Distribution

As ID professionals we take pride in our ability to conduct front-end analyses, design curricula, and develop effective instructional materials. In other words, we tend to identify most with the activities which make up Phase II of the model. So when our projects move into Phase III: Follow Up, we often begin to lose interest. When we hear the words reproduction and distribution, we immediately think, "delegate!" We'd much rather move on to a new project. After all, we've been involved in the production sessions and have personally seen to it that the master materials are perfect. It feels like our work is done.

Yet our ultimate "customers," the students and instructors who will be using our courseware, will never see those lovely master materials.

ID Project Management

They will instead receive copies that have, in many cases, been created by people who have had little involvement with the project to date. These reproduction and distribution people must see to it that color emphasis is placed precisely on pages, three-ring binders and tab dividers are put together properly, cassette labels are accurate, the right quantities are packaged and sent to each training location, and so on. Foul-ups in these seemingly "minor details" can cause confusion and frustration for both students and instructors.

In short, if instructional materials are improperly reproduced or distributed, all the time and money invested in development could be wasted as the class falls apart during its implementation. To prevent this from happening, you, as project manager, should make sure reproduction and distribution receive as much attention as the rest of the project.

The results you should achieve during reproduction and distribution are fairly clear-cut. Step 8: Reproduce, should result in high-quality copies of all course materials, as embodied in the masters that were approved by your sponsor. Step 9: Distribute, should result in the dissemination of these materials to training and storage sites.

It's true that dealing with the many details involved in achieving these results could make you crazy. But if you take these activities one step at a time, they can be entirely manageable.

Your Role as Manager

To assure that materials are reproduced and distributed properly, the project manager should perform these sub-steps:

- Orient reproduction and distribution team members to the project.

- Confirm the reproduction and distribution methods and schedules.

- Review samples of reproduced materials as they are available.

- Inspect the storage and distribution system to make sure it will work properly.

- Obtain sponsor approval of the reproduced materials and the distribution methodology.

To complete these you will need to plan carefully, stimulate the right action at the right time, and intervene as needed. The following chart summarizes this process.

Manager Role / Activity	Plan	Stimulate Action	Intervene
Orient Repro./Dist. Team	Prepare overview; Assemble approved masters	Meet with producers; Show how pieces fit together	"Sell" design strategy; Discuss team concerns
Confirm Repro./Dist. Method/Schedule	List requirements of repro./dist. method/schedule	Agree on methods and schedule with team	Defend sponsor requirements; Discuss concerns
Review Samples	Set deadlines for getting samples of each medium	Review and approve samples; Involve sponsors	Note deviations from the design; Specify revisions
Inspect Storage & Distribution System	Assemble specifications; Set up inspections	Visit storage, distribution sites; Inspect	Note deviations from plan; Specify changes
Obtain Sponsor Approval	Plan review of sample copies and distribution method	Review samples and distribution method with sponsor	Note required changes; Get signoff

Figure 9-2: Manager Activities During Reproduce & Distribute

For the sake of clarity, each of these activities is treated as if it happens solely during reproduction and distribution. However, you might want to conduct some of these activities as early as Step 4: Develop the Blueprint. In general, the earlier that these activities are conducted, the better.

Now let's examine each sub-step.

Orient Reproduction and Distribution Team

In previous chapters it was recommended that you assign one production coordinator for each medium that will be produced. For example, you might have a print production coordinator to work with the print production people, an audio-visual production coordinator to work with the video and audio producers, and so on. This can simplify your job by reducing the number of people whom you must directly coordinate. In addition, having a seasoned production specialist perform the initial inspections of the media products can help you achieve higher quality with fewer costly revisions.

In most cases, your print coordinator will be familiar with the people who handle reproduction, distribution, and storage of instructional materials for your organization. Often, these people report directly to your print coordinator either as internal staff or as outside vendors. If this is not the case in your organization, then you will need to identify these people yourself and make sure they are part of your planning efforts.

Regardless of who reports to whom, you will need to begin reproduction and distribution by holding an orientation meeting to communicate your project's requirements. This means that you must show the reproduction and distribution team how the pieces fit together and how the design strategy works. The better informed they are about your instructional intent, the more likely they are to help you achieve that intent through their efforts.

The previous chapter recommended that you hold a similar orientation meeting for print and audio-visual media producers. In some situations, it may make sense to simply combine these two orientation sessions into one meeting for all the members of the production, reproduction, and distribution team.

Confirm Reproduction/Distribution Method and Schedule

After team members have been oriented to your project, you will need to negotiate specific reproduction and distribution methods. For example, will print materials be photo-copied or offset printed? And how will the materials be assembled into the finished package? And how many copies will be sent to the training sites as compared to storage sites? These are the kinds of questions that must be discussed before reproduction and distribution can begin.

As project manager, your role in these discussions is to represent your ultimate constituents, the students and instructors who will be using the materials. You must make sure that the reproduction methods will support the instructional intent of the training, while the distribution and storage methods will make the course easy to administer. These discussions can often initiate "territorial disputes," such as who will pay for shipping, whose office space will be used for storage, and whose staff will be responsible for assembling materials for each class session. Therefore, it may be appropriate for the sponsor to be present at these discussions to help mediate disputes.

After you have decided on the reproduction and distribution methods, you will need to develop a detailed schedule. It is assumed that the overall project schedule you have been using to this point has broad time frames set aside for reproduction and distribution. However, now it's time to negotiate a detailed schedule. Your role as project manager is to present your "firm" deadline requirements and then help the reproduction and distribution team figure out how to meet them.

Beginning on the next page are some guidelines for orienting reproduction and distribution people and helping establish the schedule.

Review Samples

Reproducing master materials is typically time-consuming and expensive. That's why it's important to check samples of the reproductions before the entire reproduction run is completed. In some cases, this will require that you or the course designer be on site, at the reproduction facility, as the first copies of each component are completed. This will help assure that time and money aren't wasted on inappropriate reproduction techniques.

Specifically, you should set deadlines for reviewing samples of all the different types of deliverables that are being reproduced. For example, your print reproduction person should provide you with a sample workbook page, a sample instructor page, a sample job aid, and samples of other types of print materials after the first few copies are made. Your A-V reproduction person can provide you with samples of audio or video tape copies.

When you or your designer have approved the samples, you might ask your sponsor to look at them and note any required revisions. After everyone on the design team approves the samples, the reproduction people can continue their work secure in the knowledge that they have the support of the rest of the design team.

The Reproduction Evaluation Checklist provides some tips on what to look for when reviewing sample reproductions. In addition, Typical Reproduction and Distribution Checkpoints is a worksheet that can help set dates for these reviews.

Guidelines for the Reproduction and Distribution Orientation Meeting

The following guidelines may be used to help plan your orientation meeting with reproduction and distribution people.

Before you start the meeting:

☐ Obtain any reproduction and distribution guidelines or standards which your organization imposes on training media.

For example, all print media must be shrink-wrapped and include a letter from the Vice President of Training welcoming students to the course. Or all shipping of course materials must be by five-day ground transport, unless more costly next day air shipping is approved in writing by the department head.

☐ Assemble samples of reproduced and packaged materials (other courseware) that are similar to what you or your sponsor has in mind.

☐ Assemble the master materials for each course component (workbooks, job aids, computer disks, video tapes, etc.), along with a list of how many copies of each component will be needed.

☐ Assemble your schedule requirements (deadlines) for having materials distributed and ready for the first training session.

☐ Prepare an overview presentation that describes the "big picture" of the course you are creating and outlines the way reproduction and distribution methods will support the course goals.

At the meeting:

☐ Describe how the pieces fit together and what trainees will be doing when using them. (Knowing the context in which materials will be used can help reproduction and distribution people produce more effective solutions.)

☐ Get excited about the design strategy and let your enthusiasm show. "Sell" it, if necessary.

☐ Show the samples of what you want and relate them to the master materials produced so far and your organization's reproduction and distribution guidelines.

- [ ] State exactly how many units of each course component you will need immediately and how many should be placed in storage.

- [ ] Describe which reproduction and distribution decisions are firm (sponsor requirements that aren't negotiable) and which are open for suggestion.

- [ ] Present your schedule requirements and any firm deadlines.

- [ ] Answer questions and discuss team members' concerns.

- [ ] Get agreement on reproduction and distribution methods and a detailed schedule. [See Sample Reproduction and Distribution Checkpoints.]

After the meeting:

- [ ] Document the agreements in writing in a project status report. (See Chapter 3: How to Organize the Project for an example.)

- [ ] Send copies of the status report to all project players, including the sponsor.

- [ ] Make sure everyone on the project team gets a copy of the negotiated reproduction and distribution schedule.

Reproduction Evaluation Checklist

When evaluating samples of reproduced materials, consider these typical criteria, then discuss any problems in the materials with your reproduction people.

Print Materials

☐ Are "second colors" reproduced properly? (Check by comparing to the "blue lines" or "brown lines.")

☐ Is there "color shift" or fading from one sample to the next?

☐ Does print "bleed through" from one page to another?

☐ Are photos clean, crisp, and not muddy?

☐ Are graphics, especially those with fine detail, crisp and legible? Are call-outs (arrows, highlighting, etc.) accurate?

☐ Do bindings, tabs, covers, or other packaging conflict with or support the instructional message?

☐ Are the pages in assembled binders properly collated?

☐ Are printed labels for audio-visual, computer disk, or other media clean and easy to read?

☐ If intended, does the printing style of media labels match the other print materials?

Audio-Visual Media

☐ Are there "slates" at the beginning of audio and video tapes that fully identify the production?

☐ Are multi-part media productions clear and easy to use?

For example, is a six-part audio tape adventure contained on one long tape or on six short tapes? Do tape labels help clarify their use or cause confusion? Does the packaging help keep the pieces together? The answers to these questions will depend on your unique instructional design.

- [ ] Are slides or overhead transparencies clearly labeled so they can be assembled quickly if they are dropped and thrown out of sequence?

- [ ] Are slides or overhead transparencies crisp, containing all the detail and emphasis as planned?

- [ ] Do audio tapes contain thumps, hums, whistles, or other sounds that would indicate poor quality reproduction?

- [ ] Do video tapes contain "snow," do colors "bloom," or are there lines on the screen that weren't present on the master tapes?

- [ ] Do the audio portions of video tapes contain thumps, hums, or whistles?

General

- [ ] Do the reproduced materials match or exceed the masters in quality?

- [ ] If there are deviations from specifications, does the sponsor approve?

Sample Reproduction and Distribution Checkpoints

Below are some typical checkpoints that can serve as deadlines during reproduction and distribution of print and audio-visual materials. Specific dates should be assigned to each.

Date: **Checkpoint:**

_____   Reproduction/distribution team orientation meeting completed

_____   Final masters reviewed by sponsor, approved, and delivered to reproduction facilities *

_____   Sample of each reproduced component provided to ID and sponsor for review and approval *

_____   Sample packaging provided to ID and sponsor for review and approval *

_____   Decision finalized on storage site for extra copies

_____   Decision finalized on distribution methodology (who will distribute to what locations via what means on what dates)

_____   Enough reproduced materials ready for first session of course

_____   All materials reproduced in sufficient quantities for storage

_____   Storage and distribution methodology completed and operational

---

* NOTE: It may be useful to set separate deadlines for delivery of each media component. For example, laminated job aids might be ready on a different date than audio cassettes or workbook pages.

Inspect Storage and Distribution System

As a rule, you can achieve substantial savings by reproducing course materials in large quantities. This is because the time and money expended in setting up reproduction and packaging equipment will be the same whether you are printing 50 copies or 5000 copies. By spreading these set-up costs over a large quantity of materials, the cost per copy can be considerably reduced. That's the good news.

The bad news, however, is that after you have all these copies you must store them someplace and then make sure they are distributed to your training sites as needed. This can get pretty complicated, especially if you have a lot of training sites scattered around the country. So it's worthwhile for you to inspect the storage and distribution system to make sure it will do the job for you.

Before you conduct this inspection, you should assemble your distribution specifications as negotiated earlier in the orientation meeting. Then set up appointments with the people who will handle storage and distribution and make on-site inspections of their facilities. During the visits, note ways in which the system seems to deviate from specifications and then negotiate improvements.

Does this on-site inspection sound like overkill? Consider this example. In one situation an on-site inspection revealed that beautiful, custom-crafted courseware was "dumped" in the corner of a storage closet, audio cassettes falling out of the binders, with no one quite sure where the video tapes and overheads were located. No wonder instructors had trouble finding what they needed to conduct the course! You can be certain that it was easy to negotiate some improvements in that particular storage and distribution system.

Of course, your particular requirements will differ from project to project. The following checklist has some things you might consider when conducting your inspection.

Important Features of a Storage and Distribution System

Below are key features of a storage or distribution system for course materials.

Storage System

- [ ] Temperature, humidity, physical arrangement of shelves, etc., will help prolong the life of materials.

- [ ] Adequate security will prevent unauthorized use of materials.

- [ ] Security is not an obstacle for instructors and students who want to obtain materials.

- [ ] Storage sites are located close enough to the classroom so materials can be obtained quickly and easily.

- [ ] Storage people know how many copies of materials must be stored, for how long, and when these copies will be arriving.

- [ ] Storage people are aware of who will be contacting them for copies and when they will be doing so.

- [ ] The storage method is a part of the distribution system; storage people report to the distribution people.

Distribution System

- [ ] There are policies and/or procedures in place that describe:
  - What specific steps must be taken to obtain materials.
  - Who is authorized to request and obtain materials.
  - Who is responsible for shipping or delivering materials.
  - What shipping method (specific carrier) should be used.
  - How much advance notice is required for shipments.

- [ ] Distribution people have specific names, addresses, and phone numbers of people in training sites who will receive materials.

- [ ] Distribution people have specific quantities of which materials will be needed in which training sites at which specific dates.

- [ ] Distribution people have ongoing communication with reproduction people and the project manager to clarify their tasks.

Obtain Sponsor Approval

The final task in reproducing and distributing course materials is to obtain your sponsor's approval.

To get this approval, you need to plan a meeting in which you will show the sponsor a finished set of reproduced materials. You should also plan to walk the sponsor through the specifics of the distribution system. If appropriate, you might plan to have members of the reproduction and distribution team attend the meeting to clarify potentially confusing issues.

At the meeting, you should review the finished set of materials by browsing through the pages of print materials, playing or showing any media, and focusing the sponsor's attention on the quality of the reproductions. In addition, you should walk the sponsor, step-by-step, through the distribution system that will be used to store and disseminate copies of the course. As with previous approval sessions, you should note changes that are requested by the sponsor and then obtain his or her written approval (sign-off) on this step of the project.

CAUTION: If you wait until all copies of the materials have been made before you review sample copies with the sponsor, you risk having to redo everything if the sponsor has major objections. Therefore, you should have your sponsor review and approve samples of reproductions well before the entire reproduction run is completed.

Conclusion

This chapter has described how to manage Step 8: Reproduce and Step 9: Distribute. In particular, it has provided some techniques for orienting reproduction and distribution people to the project and for negotiating reproduction and distribution methods and schedules. In addition, it provided some suggestions for what to look for when reviewing samples of reproduced media and when inspecting a storage and distribution system. Finally, it examined how to obtain your sponsor's approval for these steps of the project.

The next chapter will describe some techniques for managing the last step of the project management process, Step 10: Evaluate.

Chapter 10

How to Manage Follow-Up Evaluation

The first chapter of this book presented a typical ID project management model and an overview of the project manager's job in implementing the model. The next two chapters discussed Phase I of the model, Project Planning, including Step 1: Determine Project Scope and Step 2: Organize the Project. The next five chapters presented information on Phase II of the model, Instructional Development. In particular, these chapters reviewed some techniques for managing Step 3: Gather Information, Step 4: Develop the Blueprint, Step 5: Create Draft Materials, Step 6: Test Draft Materials, and Step 7: Produce Master Materials. Finally, the preceding chapter shifted our focus to Phase III: Follow Up. In particular, some techniques for managing Step 8: Reproduce and Step 9: Distribute were presented.

In this, the final chapter of the book, we will examine some methods for organizing and managing Step 10: Evaluate.

Two Assumptions

The purpose of Step 10: Evaluate is to determine the long-term effectiveness of the instructional materials that were created during earlier ID activities. At this point we make two assumptions:

- **The materials to be evaluated are performance-based.** That is, there are specified skill or knowledge objectives that serve as targets for student performance. If there are no performance objectives, the evaluation techniques discussed here will not make sense.

- **Time, money, people, and other resources will be available** to make the improvements recommended by the evaluation. If there will be no resources available to implement the recommendations, then the evaluation is a waste of effort.

Caution: Seek Expert Advice

A note of caution: It's true that nearly every instructional developer at some time or another must evaluate instructional materials. However, bear in mind that evaluation is a discrete discipline, intimately related to, but separate from, instructional development. If you are fortunate enough to have access to evaluation professionals, then you should get their advice when planning and conducting evaluations. If, like most of us, you must develop your evaluation strategy without input from such specialists, then you should proceed with caution.

In any case, this chapter will not attempt to provide detailed instructions for conducting evaluations. There are plenty of other texts that are devoted solely to this topic. Instead, we will focus on what the project manager can do to ensure that the evaluation is as effective as possible.

About Follow-Up Evaluation

In an article entitled *Levels of Evaluation*, Valorie Beer and Anne Bloomer argue that the usual distinction between formative and summative evaluation is not particularly helpful for planning evaluations. Instead, they recommend that evaluation efforts be categorized into three different levels, each of which contains elements of formative and summative evaluation. [Author's note: It is strongly suggested that project managers examine Beer and Bloomer's article. It sorts out some major issues associated with evaluation and discusses instrumentation and methods in clear terms. It helped inspire much of this chapter.]

These levels of evaluation, along with the questions asked by each, are loosely summarized below:

Level One evaluation identifies required revisions prior to implementation. It asks:

- Is the training working as it was designed to work?

Level Two evaluation describes the effectiveness of the course after implementation. It asks:

- Are students achieving the objectives?
- Are student needs being met by the program?

Level Three evaluation examines both the effectiveness and the overall relevance of the course. It asks:

- Are skills, knowledge, and attitudes being transferred to the real world?

- What are the problems in achieving transfer and what are some solutions?

- Are the course objectives really relevant?

Chapter 7, How to Test Draft Materials, dealt primarily with what Beer and Bloomer would call Level One evaluation. That is, the purpose of testing draft materials is to determine whether the training works and what revisions are needed before implementation.

On the other hand, follow-up evaluation, the topic of this chapter, occurs after the course is implemented. Such evaluations attempt to answer Level Two or Level Three questions. In order to answer such complex questions, it's necessary to gather data from many different sources. Therefore, this type of evaluation effort is a project unto itself, requiring its own project strategy and checkpoints.

Typical Tasks in Follow-Up Evaluation

Follow-up evaluation typically involves these broad tasks:

- **Define the objectives** of the evaluation and select an appropriate evaluation strategy.

- **Develop the tools** (surveys, observation guides, etc.) needed to execute the strategy.

- **Implement the strategy** and gather data as planned.

- **Synthesize,** analyze, and summarize the data.

- **Report the results** of the evaluation and make recommendations based on the results.

Figure 10-1 illustrates the flow of these tasks and shows the typical outputs of each.

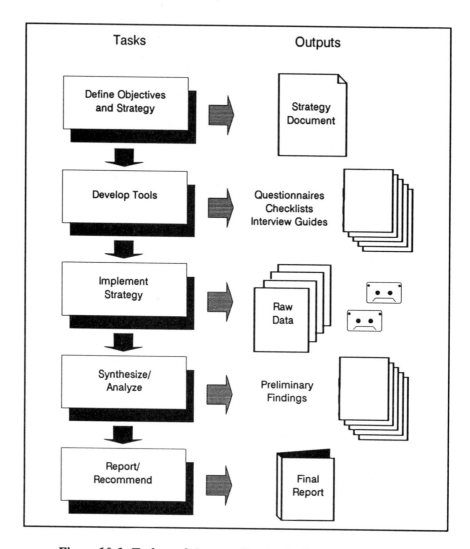

Tasks | Outputs

Define Objectives and Strategy → Strategy Document

Develop Tools → Questionnaires Checklists Interview Guides

Implement Strategy → Raw Data

Synthesize/ Analyze → Preliminary Findings

Report/ Recommend → Final Report

Figure 10-1: Tasks and Outputs During Follow-Up Evaluation

As you can see, each task in the evaluation effort results in a specific output that, in turn, helps to build a foundation for the next output.

As project manager, it's your job to help plan each of these tasks, stimulate action by the evaluation team to get the job done, and intervene as needed to keep things moving.

Figure 10-2 summarizes these manager activities.

Manager Role / Activity	Plan	Stimulate Action	Intervene
Define Objectives & Strategy	Discuss with sponsor, consumers of training	Meet with team; Determine objectives & strategy	Keep team focused on key issues
Develop Tools	Set deadlines; Provide samples	Review and approve tools; Involve sponsor	Note deviations from strategy; Specify changes
Implement Strategy	Schedule observations, interviews, etc.	Observe evaluation team in action	Note deviations from strategy; Get back on track
Synthesize & Analyze	Set deadlines; Remind team of key objectives	Meet with team; Review patterns, supporting data	Keep team focused on evaluation objectives
Report & Recommend	Provide team with report outline; Confirm deadlines	Review and approve draft report; Present to sponsor	Discuss sponsor concerns; Clarify and revise

Figure 10-2: Manager Activities During Follow-Up Evaluation

Now let's examine each of these more closely.

Define Objectives and Select a Strategy

Shortly after your evaluation team is assembled, you will need to define the objectives of the evaluation and determine an appropriate strategy. As project manager, you can help to plan for this activity. In particular, you can talk with the sponsor and other important consumers of the training (managers of the trainees or customers who interact with trainees, for example) and determine what questions they would like the evaluation to answer. If you know their objectives and concerns, you can help shape the evaluation strategy accordingly.

Next, you should meet with the evaluation team and outline some clear, specific objectives for the evaluation. Based on these objectives, you can create a sensible strategy for executing the evaluation. The strategy should describe:

- The specific questions your evaluation should answer.

- The people your team must meet or observe in order to obtain data.

- Logistical support requirements (equipment for trainees or observers, classroom space, transportation, etc.)

- Specifications for questionnaires, interview guidelines, observer checklists, and so on.

Because your evaluation team will likely consist of instructional designers or evaluation specialists, there might be a tendency for them to overemphasize academic or theoretical issues in developing the evaluation strategy. Your job is to intervene when the balance shifts too far in the direction of the academic, making sure that the team focuses on key concerns of the sponsor and other training consumers.

When your evaluation strategy is completed, you should review it with your sponsor and obtain his or her approval. This approval is important, since in most cases sponsor personnel or resources will be affected by the evaluation activity and the recommendations which follow.

Develop Tools

After your strategy is completed and has been "blessed" by your sponsor, you can begin to develop the required tools to execute the strategy. Typical tools that might be built include:

- Course critique sheets for students, instructors, and other participants

- Observers' guidelines and checklists

- Questions for use in interviews and focus groups

- Criterion or performance tests (if they don't already exist) based on course objectives

Depending on your particular evaluation strategy, the tools you build will vary. But no matter what tools you build, it is essential that they be clear and easy for the members of the evaluation team to use. If the tools are confusing or subject to multiple interpretations, then you will likely get conflicting data and end up comparing apples to oranges.

As project manager you can help plan for the development of tools by providing samples for your team to examine. In addition, you will need to set specific deadlines for the completion of the draft tools.

Next, you should review and approve the tools and, if appropriate, obtain the sponsor's approval. (Sponsor approval is typically required when the evaluation project is politically sensitive. This is because your evaluation team may need to ask controversial questions that require careful positioning or that could lead to disputes in your sponsor's organization.) When you and the sponsor have specified all necessary changes to the tools, then you are ready to implement your evaluation strategy.

Implement the Strategy

Often the most difficult part of the evaluation effort is its implementation. Here are some typical things the evaluation team will need to do to implement the evaluation:

- Examine student performance on criterion tests (sometimes paper and pencil, sometimes observation of "live" performances such as role plays or hands-on exercises).

- Administer course critiques to students, instructors, and other participants.

- Conduct focus group sessions.

- Conduct face-to-face or telephone interviews.

- Administer questionnaires to students, instructors, managers of students, and others.

Most of these tasks involve interaction with many people. As project manager, it's your job to see that all these interactions are carefully orchestrated and scheduled. You may need to ask for your sponsor's support in setting meetings and temporarily rearranging the priorities of busy interview subjects.

Once the implementation of the evaluation is underway, it's your role to "spot check" the process and make sure everything is going according to plan. You might sit in on important focus group sessions and see how well your evaluation team is conforming to the plan. Naturally, in politically sensitive situations, you should keep your eyes and ears open for signs of trouble. Be prepared to intervene as needed to get things back on track.

Synthesize and Analyze

After the dust settles and all the data is gathered, it's time to synthesize and analyze the findings. This is often the most exciting part of the evaluation, the time when you begin to see patterns emerge from the mounds of data gathered. It's also the time when you find out how well your evaluation strategy worked. That is, did you answer the questions you set out to answer?

From a management perspective, however, this is a time when the project is vulnerable to schedule delays. This often happens when the evaluation team finds provocative new questions that can be answered by the data. They may need more time than planned to crunch numbers, compare variables, and pursue the answers.

On the one hand, you must try to live within your budget and schedule, so you can't allow the team to suffer "analysis paralysis." On the other hand, you should allow enough time to take advantage of the team's creativity and explore unanticipated questions that the evaluation might be able to answer. So you should be prepared to strike a balance between these two forces when you set your deadline for completing the analysis.

In any event, it's up to you to help the team plan the synthesis and analysis activities by setting a reasonable deadline and reminding them of the key issues and concerns the evaluation is meant to address. Then you must wait; give them time to work through the data and find the patterns.

Eventually, you should meet with the team and discuss their preliminary findings. Depending on the situation, you might want to involve your sponsor in this discussion. This is particularly important if your sponsor will be trying to "sell" your recommendations to higher-level management. By reviewing the team's preliminary findings before the final report is written, the sponsor may be able to help the team position the recommendations so that they can be implemented more smoothly.

Whether you involve the sponsor or not, your role as manager is to keep the team focused on the objectives of the evaluation by observing and intervening as needed.

Report and Recommend

The final task to be performed in the evaluation is to report the findings and make recommendations for improvement.

As project manager, you might want to help the team plan the report by providing them with a sample report outline. This will clarify your expectations. In addition, you should confirm the deadline for the report's completion.

Like any complex document, the evaluation report should include only summaries of key issues in the main body; detailed supporting data should be relegated to attachments or appendices. Charts, graphics, and tables summarizing trends in the data should be used whenever possible. Authors of the report should keep in mind the kinds of decisions that the readers of the report will be trying to make. In most cases, these readers will welcome brief summaries and clear recommendations; details and supporting data, while essential to the eventual defense of the recommendations, will be of less immediate interest to them.

Often the most effective way to present the report is with an accompanying oral presentation. Such a presentation, when supported with appropriate media and graphics, can stimulate a discussion of complex and subtle issues that can't be easily addressed in the written report.

Following the presentation of the report to the sponsor, you may need to clarify sponsor concerns and revise the report.

Conclusion

This chapter has described how to manage Step 10: Evaluate. In particular, it has provided some tips on working with the evaluation team to define objectives and strategies, develop tools, and implement the strategies. In addition, it provided some broad suggestions for managing the analysis of the evaluation data and for making the final evaluation report.

Some Final Thoughts

This brings to a close our book on ID project management. Throughout, we have attempted to provide some practical suggestions for managing the complex and difficult process of instructional development. We have provided lots of matrices, charts, and checklists to help keep this unwieldy process organized. But effective project management involves more than simply attending to these project details. To be a successful project manager, you need to have some broad general operating principles that will help you to meet the unforeseen problems that every project inevitably faces.

So in closing, we'd like to share three broad management principles that have served us quite well over the years. They are:

- Principle 1: **Hire the best people you can.**

- Principle 2: **Get the trivia out of their way.**

- Principle 3: **Plan and replan daily.**

Here's why we think these principles are so important.

Hire the Best People You Can

When you hire the best people you can, many of your project management problems will take care of themselves. Good people know what needs to be done, have the initiative to do it without asking, and can help you anticipate and handle problems before they occur. Good instructional designers, in particular, have the skill and background to perform many of the first-line management tasks that are so critical to keeping SMEs, sponsors, and media people working together as a team. So hire the best, most seasoned veterans you can afford.

Get the Trivia Out of Their Way

Good instructional design professionals are valuable resources. Yet project managers often allow IDs to waste their time performing clerical duties, engaging in battles between SMEs and the sponsor, or writing materials that are based on inaccurate documentation. These are just a few examples of the kind of "administrivia" in which IDs can become ensnared. As project manager, you should eliminate this kind of trivia so your IDs can do the work they were trained to do. So if there's not enough clerical support, it's up to you to get it. If the SMEs and the sponsor are feuding, it's up to you to try to end the dispute. And if documentation or SMEs prove inadequate, then stop the project until your team gets what it needs.

After all, if you don't eliminate the trash, who will?

Plan and Replan Daily

Every ID project is a living, swirling mass of content, deadlines, objectives, budget constraints, and changing expectations. Yesterday's plan is likely to be outdated by the events of today. So to be an effective ID project manager you need to revisit the plan nearly every day and decide if it is still relevant. If the plan needs fixing, then change it, and communicate the changes to the team.

With some common sense, the help of the principles above, and the tools and techniques described earlier in this book, you should be well equipped to succeed at managing instructional development.

Reference:

Beer, Valorie & Bloomer, Anne (1986). Levels of Evaluation. *Educational Evaluation and Policy Analysis, 8*(4), Winter, 335-345.

Appendix A

Working with Vendors

Earlier in this text, we presented a 10-Step ID Project Management Model and provided a detailed discussion of what the ID project manager should be doing to plan, stimulate action, and intervene during each of the steps. In Chapter 3, How to Organize the Project, we presented some guidelines for selecting members of the project team. (See "Who's Who on Your Project Team: A Reference Aid.") We made no distinction between team members who are full-time members of the organization (i.e., employees) and those who are contracted as vendors or outside contractors. Yet often these contracted members of the design team are essential if the project is to be successful.

In this appendix, we will present some considerations and guidelines for selecting and working with vendors.

What Is a Vendor, Anyway?

In this text, we define a **vendor** as *any individual or organization who is contracted to perform specific duties related to the project.* A vendor may be hired to produce a video tape, for example. In this case, the vendor would likely be responsible for hiring set designers, camera people, grips, lighting people, script writers, and many other professionals. While all these people are involved in the production, we would contract with a single vendor organization, let's say XYZ Video Productions, in order to get the video produced. XYZ Video would, in turn, hire or subcontract with all the professionals needed to assemble the production crew and complete the video.

An alternative is for us to contract with a specific individual. For example, we might set up a contract with Mary Smith to provide instructional development services or with John Doe to provide evaluation services. While Mary or John will not be hiring anyone else to help them fulfill our contract, we would still refer to them as our vendors.

Some organizations distinguish between vendors and contractors. For them, a vendor is defined as a company that employs several people. The term contractor, on the other hand, is reserved to describe a single individual with whom they contract.

In this text, however, we will use the word vendor to refer to either an individual or an organization with whom we establish a contract. We will use the term subcontractor to refer to those people who are contracted by the vendor.

In most locales, it is possible to contract with vendors to perform every aspect of our instructional development project. We can contract with IDs, writers, typists, graphic artists, print producers, video producers, proofreaders, ID project managers, SMEs, and on and on. We can contract for their services by the hour, by the day, by the week, or at a fixed rate for a specific project deliverable. So, given enough money and the proper project configuration, there are nearly unlimited opportunities to work with vendors.

Four Types of Vendors

The development of the personal computer and other technologies like the FAX machine and modem communications has enabled individual consultants to provide their clients with a much broader range of services than anyone would have dreamed possible as little as ten years ago. An individual consultant, equipped with powerful PC hardware and the latest software, is capable of single-handedly providing sophisticated project planning and tracking services, writing and word processing, graphic production, desktop publishing, creation of computer assisted instruction, and even some kinds of media production and editing. In effect, what formerly required a complete organization may now be accomplished by a single individual.

With each independent consultant potentially able to provide such a wide range of services, a new complexity has been introduced into the vendor selection process. In the age of the computerized independent contractor, what services does the large organization provide that aren't provided by the one-person shop?

This section describes four different classifications of vendor and illustrates how these organizations differ in terms of size and services provided. These classifications include:

- The large national vendor
- The large regional vendor
- The vendor adhocracy
- The independent consultant

The Large National Vendor

The large national vendor typically has its headquarters office located in a major city, with several regional offices in other cities around the country. Usually the regional offices are strategically located to serve the vendor's major accounts or to take advantage of the presence of specific industries. Operating out of each of these regional offices are salespeople, often called "account representatives," who have responsibility for bringing in business within their territory. In addition, these salespeople may serve as liaisons between the vendor's team of designers and the client's staff, helping to keep the peace and to keep the project on schedule (and profitable).

The large national vendor usually has substantial physical facilities, including conference rooms, professional staff offices, word processing departments, media production facilities, and other specialized equipment. A full staff of professionals (IDs, producers, accountants, etc.) is typically on the payroll and available to support a project. These national vendors can provide the management depth that is sometimes required for large projects. They often maintain close ties with independent consultants whom they hire to supplement their internal staff or to provide specialized services.

While the people, facilities, and services provided by these national organizations can be expensive, they can provide substantial project control. For example, the development and implementation of a nation-wide training program can benefit from the use of this vendor's regional offices. Their national sales force can help provide your organization with regional sales presentations to introduce the program to your geographically dispersed employees. The vendor's regional offices can also serve as focal points for development activities and coordination of implementation efforts.

On the other hand, if your project requires a smaller development effort, it may get lost in the shuffle of this vendor's many ongoing projects. In addition, keep in mind that each of this vendor's project budgets must help to recover the overhead costs of any facilities and personnel that may experience "downtime," as well as the costs of maintaining a well-traveled sales force. If your project doesn't require their unique horsepower, then you may be paying for more vendor services than you really need.

The Large Regional Vendor

The large regional vendor typically has the same configuration as the large national vendor. This includes facilities, staff, and specialized equipment, but on a smaller scale. What makes regional vendors different from the national vendor is that they do not have offices in several cities. Instead, they work out of a single set of offices in one city.

This doesn't mean that large regional vendors don't tackle long-distance clients. On the contrary, the regional vendor is usually found bidding for many of the same contracts as the national vendor. Its sales representatives simply spend more time on the road. Or the regionals may hire salespeople from several different cities who work out of their homes or use modest sales offices. However, the main body of their professionals and support staff remains in one central location.

These vendors also provide depth of management and staffing, though often limited to one primary location. They also make extensive use of independent contractors to provide specialized services. Indeed, they often establish a solid presence far away from their home base through the use of subcontractors.

However, the large regional vendor has the same difficulties as its national counterpart in budgeting for and recovering "downtime" expenses of its staff and facilities, as well as sales force expenses. It also has the same difficulty keeping small projects as a high priority. In addition, these vendors may be stretched thin when attempting to service a national account spread among several cities.

The Vendor Adhocracy

Alvin Toffler coined the word "adhocracy" to refer to an organization that is formed for one purpose only and is disbanded after that purpose is achieved. The vendor adhocracy is a team of independent consultants who are pulled together by its sponsor to complete a particular project. Often, the members of the vendor adhocracy are former staff members of regional or national vendor organizations who are now working out of their own "electronic cottages" or homes equipped with the kinds of hardware and software discussed earlier.

An adhocracy is born when a sponsor identifies a large project and then asks an independent consultant to plan it and hire other consultants to help complete it. A unique, one-time-only, staff is assembled that fits specialized needs. Such adhocracies have no centralized facilities and no full-time or salaried staff. One consultant subcontracts with other consultants to provide all the services of a large regional vendor.

There are several benefits of the vendor adhocracy. First, they are usually comprised of seasoned veterans who know how to get things done with very limited support. Second, they often bring a freshness and enthusiasm not found among members of large organizations which must constantly keep people working hard to cover overhead expenses or which suffer from internal political rivalries. Finally, vendor adhocracies, with substantially lower overhead costs, can often deliver their products or services at substantially less cost than their more permanent counterparts.

While staff quality, enthusiasm, and price are the strengths of the vendor adhocracy, there are at least two weaknesses. First, the lack of a centralized meeting facility, other than someone's dining room, can make it necessary for the sponsor to provide such space. Second, the vendor adhocracy has no salespeople. While a vendor project manager can provide some internal sales support, the intense sales and support activity provided by the national or regional vendors may not be available.

The Independent Consultant

Most sponsors recognize that the most important factors in selecting a vendor are the professional skills and experience of the person who will execute the project. That is why the salespeople of both the large national and regional vendors spend considerable time discussing the credentials of their staff members. Sponsors want to work with capable individuals. And successful independent consultants are quite capable, or they are soon out of business.

Unless specifically hired to perform management services, independents require that the client perform most of the project management tasks. The independent consultant is usually hired to perform carefully delineated project roles. While they usually provide their own clerical support, some other support staff services may be missing.

If you have a project that is clearly defined and you have the time to provide management support, the independent consultant may be the best choice. You could save money and benefit from having considerable control over the project. On the other hand, you could find yourself faced with the responsibility of providing many of the services that are routinely provided by the other three vendors described earlier.

Which Vendor Organization Is Right for You?

In a nutshell, here are the potential services provided by the vendors discussed above:

- Offices in several cities

- Support of full time salespeople

- Substantial physical facilities

- Clerical and other support staff

- Technical support

- Project management support

- Professional expertise (IDs, media professionals, etc.)

Generally speaking, you should not hire a vendor who provides more services than you need. If you need all of the services listed above, then a large national vendor is your best bet. If you need everything except the offices in several cities, then the large regional vendor may be right for you. If you can live without the offices in several cities, the salespeople, and the vendor-provided physical facilities, then the vendor adhocracy may be your best choice. And if all you need is professional expertise, and you are willing to provide all the rest, then you should consider simply using an independent consultant.

Selecting and Managing Vendors

If you approach your vendor selection and management systematically, it is likely that they will make substantial positive contributions to your projects. Conversely, if you don't plan your use of vendors carefully, you can spend many thousands of dollars and still get poor results. To ensure good results, we recommend this six-step process for working with vendors:

- Decide if you need a vendor.

- Create a request for proposal (RFP).

- Hold a bidder's conference.

- Select the best vendor.

- Negotiate the vendor contract.

- Deal with the paperwork (purchase orders, invoices, etc.).

Let's look at each of these steps in more detail.

Decide If You Need a Vendor

Contracting with vendors can be expensive. What's more, when you acquire routine, ongoing support from vendors, you often fail to develop your own internal capabilities to do the jobs the vendors are doing. Finally, vendors can have substantial impact on the quality of your finished product and your development schedule.

So deciding whether to use vendors is an important decision. Our "Decision Aid: Do We Need a Vendor?" can help you sort through the important issues.

Create a Request for Proposal (RFP)

The Request for Proposal or RFP is your official statement to all eligible vendors regarding the services you require. Vendors use your RFP as the basis for making their proposals. It is the RFP that focuses vendor attention on critical issues and shapes vendors' first impressions of your organization and the project to be completed.

Most importantly, the RFP is the foundation upon which the vendor's relationship with your organization is built. Indeed, most contracts with vendors refer directly to the RFP as a supplemental document that legally defines the project parameters from the buyer's point of view. For these reasons, the RFP must be carefully crafted and thoughtfully reviewed before distributing it to eligible vendors.

The "Guidelines for Creating the Request for Proposal" can help you construct a fairly comprehensive RFP.

Hold a Bidder's Conference

A bidder's conference is a meeting in which you present all potential vendors with your Request for Proposal (RFP). The bidder's conference can help you concentrate all your question and answer time into one efficient meeting. In this way all the vendors get the same official story regarding the required training.

We suggest that you follow these three steps when planning and conducting your Bidder's Conference.

- Get recommendations from your peers about likely vendors.

- Plan the conference.

- Assemble potential vendors and conduct the conference.

The "Guidelines for Planning the Bidder's Conference" provide more information on each of these steps.

Select the Best Vendor

When selecting the best vendor, you need to conduct at least three important activities:

- Review your Request for Proposal (RFP) and remind yourself of what you asked of your potential vendors.

- Read each vendor proposal and compare it to your RFP.

- Apply a set of criteria to rate vendor proposals, compare them, and select the best vendor.

Our "Decision Aid: Select the Best Vendor" can help you work through this process.

Negotiate the Vendor Contract

Your primary goals in negotiating a vendor contract are listed below:

- Arrive at a clear statement of price, development schedule, payment schedule, and deliverables to be provided by the vendor.

- Make sure you understand all the fine print or special assumptions made by each party to the agreement.

- Do your best to assure that the contract will protect your organization's business interests.

Our "Guidelines for Negotiating the Vendor Contract" will help you attain these goals.

Decision Aid: Do We Need a Vendor?

Deciding whether to use a vendor consists of making two decisions:

- Do we need special expertise that only vendors have?

- If we choose to use vendors, what will be the impact on the finished product?

This decision aid will help you make these decisions.

Decision 1: Do we need special expertise that only vendors have?

A. **Review the key players** required to complete your project. (See Chapter 3, "Who's Who on Your Project Team: A Reference Aid" for descriptions of typical project players.)

B. **Answer these questions:**

☐ What specific project roles are there that cannot be filled by internal staff or services? List each role.

☐ If we don't have a person on staff who could perform the role, should we hire someone full-time?

    – Is someone with the needed expertise easily found in the job market?

    – Are we likely to get someone on board soon enough to help with the project?

    – Could the expertise of the person we hire be used in later projects?

    – Would a person we hire to fill the role be likely to accept our salary and benefits package?

If you answered "yes" to most of these questions, then it may be worth searching for a new employee instead of contracting with a vendor.

If you answered "no" to these questions, move on to the next questions.

C.   **Check the problems** that you now have:

☐ No one available in-house to perform the role required

☐ A need for specialized expertise that cannot be purchased in a full-time employee or could not be used more than one time

☐ A need for specialized equipment, facilities, and technicians which we don't have available

If you checked any of the problems above, then you should consider an outside vendor.

D.   **Check the type of vendor you need.** (Remember, the more you ask the vendor to do, the higher the vendor's price will likely be.)

☐ Project planning and management

☐ Staffing of the entire team needed to create the finished deliverables

☐ Analysis of tasks and general training needs

☐ Instructional design (creating structure, format, flow of the course)

☐ Instructional development (creating materials)

☐ Script writing

☐ Stand-up delivery of instruction (a contract trainer)

☐ Creation of computer assisted instruction

☐ Print production (copy editing, layout, typesetting)

☐ Audio-visual production (video, audio, slide-tape, graphics, etc.)

☐ Reproduction and packaging of print and audio-visual materials

☐ Specialized subject matter expertise

☐ Other:

☐ Other:

> **CAUTION:** None of the areas above is labeled "Extremely fast development of materials." **Hiring a vendor to make up for a short development cycle simply doesn't make sense. It takes time for anyone, even experienced vendors, to create quality training.** If you hire a vendor knowing full-well that the development schedule is ridiculously short, you are likely to waste your money on expensive, yet necessarily substandard, training.

Decision 2: If we use vendors, what will be the impact on the finished product?

So far, you have determined that a vendor could help with your project. But before you make your final decision, you should examine the effect this could have on the quality of your finished product, your schedule, and your budget.

A.   Examine the potential impact on quality:

☐   Does the project require the creation of deliverables which couldn't have the proper point of view if created by vendors? (That is, must an internal employee, steeped in our organization's internal political climate or business environment, be the one who creates the materials?)

If so, then you should **not** consider using an outside vendor.

☐   Does the project require a particular type of deliverable (such as computer assisted instruction or video) which no one on staff has ever created?

☐   Does the project require the creation of deliverables of a quality currently unattainable by our organization?

If yes to either of these, then you may need to hire a vendor.

B.   Examine the potential impact on the schedule:

☐   Is the schedule so tight that you don't have enough time to go through the process of soliciting and reviewing bids and getting vendors up to speed on the technical content?

If so, you may need to avoid using a vendor.

☐   Does the schedule require that the project start at a time before internal people will be available?

If so, you may be forced to use a vendor team.

☐   Does the schedule require that several elements of the course be developed at the same time?

If this is so, and you don't have enough staff members available, then you may need to assemble a vendor team.

C.   **Consider hiring one or more individual vendors and managing them yourself.**

If you are able to manage the project yourself and wish to put together your own team of independent contractors, perform these steps:

☐   *First,* review your worksheet, "Estimating Project Costs" (see Chapter 2) to see how much the project will cost to develop in-house.

☐   *Second,* fill out another worksheet inserting the following estimated costs (or substitute your own estimates) for Daily Pay Rate:

Vendor manager:	$600 - 1200
Vendor developer:	$400 - 800

[Note: Expect to add an extra 10 to 25% to the vendor's total cost if you choose to pay the vendor a fixed price for the whole contract. Rates above are for vendor contracts in which they are paid by the number of days expended (time and materials).]

☐   *Third,* compare the costs of developing in-house versus using outside vendors.

D.   **Consider having vendor organizations handle the project on a "turn-key" basis.**

If you can't assemble the team and manage the team yourself, consider having vendor organizations make competitive, fixed-price bids for completion of the entire project. To estimate how much they are likely to charge, do the following:

☐   *First,* talk to your manager or peers to determine if they have ever used an outside vendor to complete a similar project. If so, ask how much the vendor was paid. (Note especially contract cost overruns or other financial problems.)

☐   *Next,* find out the prices quoted by some of the viable competitors for the project.

☐   *Finally,* compare these prices to the cost of developing in-house.

E.   **Examine the security risk.** (For example, will having vendors in the building at late hours present a risk? Or will having vendors learn about our new product or process pose a security risk?)

F.   **Examine the potential ROA** (return on assets) that is diminished by continuous reliance on outside vendors.

The bottom line: Use a vendor only when it makes good business sense.

Guidelines for Creating the Request for Proposal (RFP)

This set of guidelines provides an outline of the recommended sections of a Request for Proposal (RFP) and a brief definition of each section. Use this tool as a guide when building and evaluating your own RFP.

The General Training Need

This section should describe the general business goals that are served by the new product or process on which the training will be based. In addition, it should describe the key components of the new product or process (how it works) and compare these to existing products or processes. (Tell what's new.)

The Target Population

This section should include brief summaries of the jobs of all people who are to be trained. It should describe how their responsibilities will change as a result of the introduction of the new product or process. Numbers of people to be trained, by job category and geographic location, should be included.

Terminal Performance Objectives (TPOs)

This should describe exactly what the target population will be required to do as a result of going through the training. Each TPO should be listed. These will likely be preliminary. If appropriate, invite the vendor to evaluate and propose alternative TPOs.

Constraints on Budget, Schedule, and Design

This section should describe how much money is available to spend with the vendor on this project. In addition, it should include specific dates for: completion of the analysis*, blueprint, drafts, test session, master deliverables, and reproduced copies. It should also outline implementation plans (locations, dates, types and numbers of instructors, etc.). Finally, it should include constraints on the design such as your requirement to have the vendor develop the training in a self-study format, on videodisc, or whatever.

---

* This assumes that you are requesting that the vendor complete the analysis. You might consider doing the analysis yourself.

Resources Available

This section should describe the resources to be provided by your organization. Specifically, it should include a description of the subject matter experts, market research, technical documentation, equipment or facilities, and any other resources that will be available for the vendor during the development process.

Criteria for Selecting a Vendor

This is a list of the criteria which will be used to determine the best vendor proposal. Typical criteria include: vendor quality as evidenced in samples of work, vendor price, vendor's understanding of the subject matter, track record within your organization, quality of proposed solution, creative use of media, and so on. If you intend to use a weighting method (for example, assign twice as much value to creative use of media as you assign to price) then describe this to the vendor. (See also Decision Aid: Select the Best Vendor.)

The Required Development Process

This section should list each step of the development process that the vendor will be expected to perform. In addition, it should list the specific deliverables resulting from the completion of that step.

Requests for Vendor Suggestion or Creativity

This includes areas in which you are uncertain and seek recommendations or areas in which you are flexible regarding design. Vendors are usually experienced professionals who are capable of conceiving of several creative alternatives. However, if your RFP leaves the vendor with the impression that you have already locked in on a specific mode of instruction (self-study, driven by slide-tape, for example), the vendor is not likely to propose something drastically different.

Therefore, you should openly state those areas in which you are flexible or seek vendor recommendations.

How and When to Respond

This should tell the vendor how many copies of the proposal are due to whom, at what location, on what dates, and so on. Finally, it should invite vendors to make a formal presentation of their proposal, if appropriate.

Guidelines for Planning the Bidder's Conference

Complete the following steps to plan and conduct the bidder's conference.

Step 1: Ask your peers to recommend likely vendors.

Check with people in your organization who have used vendors before. If no one in your organization has ever used vendors, then contact members of your local chapters of NSPI (National Society for Performance and Instruction), ASTD (American Society for Training and Development), or other professional training organizations.

When you are seeking information and recommendations about vendors, ask these kinds of questions:

☐ Specifically what has the vendor produced that is similar in subject matter or delivery mode to the project that you are planning? (Get samples and evaluate them, if possible.)

☐ Has the vendor had trouble meeting project deadlines? If so, why?

☐ Does the vendor have the ability to "run with the ball" when given responsibility, or does the vendor require constant supervision?

☐ Does the vendor have unnecessary people on his/her team who require time and effort to deal with? (For example, will you have to deal with superfluous management or salespeople?)

☐ Does the vendor have good interpersonal skills, enabling him/her to deal with other members of the project team, as well as sponsors, SMEs, and reviewers?

☐ Would you use this vendor again? Why or why not?

Step 2: Plan the bidder's conference.

The bidder's conference should be planned in the following manner:

A. **Contact several vendors** by phone and then by follow-up letter and explain, briefly, the time and place of the session.

☐ Expect to spend no more than two hours at the meeting. In this time, you will present vendors with the RFP and answer questions.

Optionally, you might want to send out the RFP ahead of time so vendors may review it in detail before the conference. This way they can mull it over and bring their questions with them.

☐ The meeting should be held in a closed conference room, with refreshments if desired.

☐ In the introductory letter and phone call, be careful to disclose no confidential information. Also, do not give one vendor more information than another.

B. **Invite your immediate supervisor or sponsor or SMEs** to attend the meeting if you anticipate vendor questions which would require discussion by upper management or technical people.

C. **Assemble the following:**

☐ Copies of the **RFP**.

☐ Any **visual aids** which might be useful in explaining the product or process.

System flow diagrams, exploded diagrams of components, and other visuals might help vendors become familiar with the product or process quickly.

☐ **Non-disclosure agreements** for all vendors to sign, if applicable, to assure secrecy when describing confidential products or processes.

Such agreements require vendors to acknowledge in writing that they are receiving information that is secret or proprietary and that they will not disclose this information to anyone. In addition, the agreement should require that each vendor return all documentation or other background information you provide them about the project and refrain from making or circulating copies.

Step 3: *Assemble potential vendors and conduct the bidder's conference.*

At the bidder's conference, make sure you do the following:

☐ Require all vendors to sign the non-disclosure agreement before discussing details of the product/process or the project.

☐ Provide each vendor with the RFP and point out the deadline for response.

☐ Review the RFP, focusing on controversial or potentially difficult topics.

☐ Make sure you help to keep the proposed vendor solutions within the parameters established by highlighting the section of your RFP describing constraints on budget, schedule, and design.

☐ Explain and justify to vendors your required development model and training requirements.

Especially discuss how this process affects vendor deliverables, review and approval points, and vendor payment.

☐ Provide all vendors with the same information.

This means that if a vendor approaches you after the session is formally over (as often happens) and asks you about a critical piece of information, you should make sure all other potential vendors get this information before submitting their proposals.

Decision Aid: Select the Best Vendor

This decision aid can help you select the best vendor for the job. It assumes that you have written a Request for Proposal (RFP) and have distributed it to at least two potential vendors who have, in turn, submitted proposals describing their recommendations for completing your project.

Step 1. Review Your Request for Proposal (RFP)

Before you begin to choose the best vendor, you need to refresh your memory regarding the contents of your RFP. Briefly review it so you are familiar with what you asked of all vendors.

Step 2. Read Each Vendor Proposal and Compare to RFP

With your RFP clearly in mind, examine each vendor proposal. In particular, look for answers to these broad questions:

☐ Does the vendor understand our development process?

☐ Does the vendor understand our project requirements? (Are all required deliverables, constraints, etc., accounted for?)

☐ Does the vendor list any assumptions or "fine print" that should be clarified? For example,

- Are there penalty fees for schedule delays?

- Is the vendor assuming we will provide specific equipment or facilities?

- Is the vendor assuming "first priority" availability of our SMEs or other reviewers?

☐ Are we certain that the ID professionals who wrote the proposal and attended initial vendor "sales" meetings will be the same people who will work on our project? (In other words, are there ghost writers or unacknowledged student assistants in the vendor shop who will be used to execute the project? Should we "get it in writing" that the people who wrote the proposal will also be developing our training?)

Step 3. Apply Criteria to Rate Vendor Proposals and Compare

Your RFP should have clearly described your criteria for vendor selection. Now it's time to apply these criteria to compare vendors. Below is a worksheet containing typical criteria that could be used to compare two vendors.

Follow these steps to use this worksheet:

A. Review the "Vendor Selection Criteria" below and change them as needed to fit your project.

B. Review the "Possible Points" listed for each criterion and change them to reflect your own weighting scale.

C. Choose two vendor proposals and assign a code letter (A or B) to each. (To compare more than two vendors, make additional copies of the worksheet.)

D. Fill in the blanks for each vendor, add up their scores, and compare.

Vendor Selection Criteria:	*Possible Points:*	*Vendor A Score:*	*Vendor B Score:*
Vendor plan will meet our deadlines.	6	_____	_____
Vendor work plan will produce quality results.	6	_____	_____
Vendor plan allows us plenty of chances to review & approve.	4	_____	_____
Vendor team members are well-qualified.	6	_____	_____
Vendor team members all have solid track records.	6	_____	_____
Vendor has adequate facilities and equipment.	3	_____	_____
Vendor has adequate quality-assurance processes.	6	_____	_____
Design strategy provides for effective materials.	5	_____	_____

Vendor Selection Criteria:	Possible Points:	Vendor A Score:	Vendor B Score:
Design strategy provides for lots of student practice.	6		
Design strategy addresses student motivation.	5		
Suggested content shows vendor comprehends our need.	5		
Production recommendations are appropriate.	5		
Specific deliverables are detailed and appropriate.	6		
Vendor makes fair assumptions about our role on the project.	4		
Vendor references (former clients) provide strong recommendations.	5		
Vendor team has necessary interpersonal skills.	5		
Vendor team members are familiar with content.	4		
Vendor will likely need little "hand holding."	5		
Other:	2		
Other:	2		
Other:	2		
Other:	2		
TOTAL POINTS:	100		

Guidelines for Negotiating the Vendor Contract

Below are some typical steps to complete the negotiation of a vendor contract:

Step 1. **Review** the price, payment schedule, terms, conditions, and deliverables presented in **the vendor's proposal.** Also review any contract prepared by the vendor, noting key vendor requirements.

Step 2. **Obtain a sample contract** from your supervisor or legal department.

Step 3. **Translate the contract and proposal presented by the vendor** into a contract that is consistent with this sample and consistent with your plans for the project.

Step 4. **Review this contract,** make sure you understand all its provisions, and **be prepared to defend** those sections that are in the best interests of your organization.

Step 5. **Meet with your supervisor or legal department representative to explain** why you agree to all of these provisions or how you think some of the provisions might be changed by the vendor.

Step 6. **Present the vendor with the contract** that you and your supervisor agree upon.

Pay special attention to these elements:

☐ Vendor understanding of what constitutes reasonable expenses above and beyond consulting fees to be paid.

☐ Vendor understanding of what will lead to the approval of invoices (sign-off prerequisites).

☐ Exact form and content of deliverables at each stage.

☐ Your understanding of all support that your organization will provide (special equipment, special SMEs, etc.).

☐ Note the expected timeframe (schedule) and termination date. Review the penalties to be sure you understand what happens if you run over the allowable timeframe. (You probably will pay a penalty fee.)

Step 7. **Discuss counter proposals** with the vendor and your supervisor.

Step 8. **Ask the vendor to review and approve the contract.**

If the vendor will not approve the contract, note vendor's concerns and return to Step 3.

Deal with the Paperwork

Your vendor is an important member of your development team. Your relationship with your vendor can be enhanced by making sure that the vendor's first invoice (and all subsequent invoices) are paid promptly.

In order to get your vendor paid, you must typically deal with lots of paperwork. In general, however, this paperwork can be divided into two broad categories:

- Paperwork related to establishing a Purchase Order (PO).

- Paperwork related to processing vendor invoices.

About Purchase Orders (POs) and Invoices

A purchase order (often referred to as a "PO") is an order from your finance department to set aside money for payment to a specific company. Consider this example: Let's say you need to use ABC Copy Shop to make copies of materials for your project. You don't expect your total cost of copies to exceed $1000 and you want the copy shop employees to be able to send you their bills, called invoices, so they can receive payment. In other words, you need to establish a $1000 pool of money that is set aside for use by ABC Copy Shop.

Your finance department sets up this pool of money and gives it a unique label, so it may be differentiated from other pools of money they have set up for paying other companies. This label takes the form of a Purchase Order (PO) number; let's say it's PO number 5243C.

The next thing you need to do is to tell ABC Copy Shop that they should include this special PO number on all their invoices (bills) that relate to this project and its corresponding PO. In this way, when the invoice gets paid, your finance department can keep track of how much money is being spent from the copy shop's pool of money.

So eventually you send out some materials to ABC Copy Shop for copying. They make your copies and send you an invoice (bill). You review the invoice, check to see that it refers to PO number 5243C, as required, you write "approved for payment" on the bottom, and you forward it to the finance department. The finance department sends a check to ABC Copy Shop in the amount of the invoice and everyone lives happily ever after.

To summarize, a Purchase Order (PO) has been established to set aside a pool of money for a particular vendor and for a particular purpose. As project manager, you review and approve the vendor invoices (bills) for payment and pass them along to the finance department. The finance department verifies that the money has been set up for the vendor's use (i.e., they verify the PO) and then they send the vendor a check. It seems simple, right?

Yet for many ID project managers, this process is difficult and time consuming. This is often because the finance department has all sorts of documentation that is required to substantiate POs and to process invoices. This documentation is sometimes difficult to assemble. Below is a list of the types of things you can expect your finance department to ask for when you are establishing a PO for a vendor and when you are processing invoices.

Typical Documentation Required to Set Up POs

In most large organizations, the finance department will likely ask project managers for the following documentation when they attempt to set up purchase orders:

- A filled-in Purchase Requisition form.

  (This is a finance department form that requests that a Purchase Order be established, thus its name "requisition." It asks for details about the project, the vendor, the total amount of money needed, etc.)

- Copy of your Request for Proposal (RFP).

- The name of the chosen vendor and why the vendor was chosen.

- The names of other vendors bidding and a statement delineating why they were not chosen.

- The vendor proposal.

- Description of work to be performed (if different from that described in the proposal).

- The agreed-upon vendor payment schedule.

- A copy of the contract with the vendor.

- Vendor name and address.

- Vendor federal ID number or Social Security number and business classification form (for tax purposes).

- Name and mail location of person filling out the Purchase Requisition (usually the ID project manager's name and address).

- Non-Disclosure Agreement, signed by vendor. (See Guidelines for Planning the Bidder's Conference, Step 2, for details.)

Getting Your Vendors Paid

As a general rule, the larger the organization, the more people will be handling the vendor invoices (bills) in order to pay vendors. You can help expedite things by making yourself an outline of the process (who handles what, when) and by developing a solid relationship with everyone in the finance department who handles POs and vendor invoices. Talk to your supervisor or finance manager and get answers to these questions:

- Who will approve your Purchase Requisition? (List all players.)

- Who can help you interpret the paperwork requirements for your unique project?

- What, specifically, are the steps involved in processing the Purchase Requisition? (List them, including names and phone numbers of everyone handling the Purchase Requisition.)

- On what date, specifically, can you expect to have a PO number? (Make a note of this date on your calendar and follow up if you have not received the PO number as promised.)

- Who will approve your vendor's invoice for payment? (List all players.)

- What, specifically, are the steps involved in processing the invoice? (List all steps and be prepared to track them.)

It's a good idea to meet in person or telephone all the people who will approve your PO requisition and your vendor's invoices. Walk them through your package of paperwork and make sure they verify that no information is missing. Ask the person who will pay the vendor on what date, specifically, the vendor can expect to receive payment. Then notify your vendor. Make a note of this date on your calendar and follow up if your vendor has not received the payment as promised.

Tracking Your Vendor's Invoices (Keeping Your Own Books)

After you have set up your contract with your vendor and have established a PO and method for getting invoices paid, it's a good idea to establish your own tracking system so you can see how your project's money is being spent. This system should be distinct from the finance department's, in that it should be simple and should allow you, as project manager, to focus on only those invoices (bills) relating to the project.

The Invoice Tracker can help.

Invoice Tracker

After you have established a contract with a vendor and have set up a Purchase Order (PO) to allow vendor payment, you will need to track vendor invoices as they are paid. Use the Invoice Tracker to track invoices and expenses against Purchase Orders. As you receive and approve invoices, simply fill in the blanks as illustrated on the sample.

Note the following definitions of blanks on the form. Compare these to the example shown on the next page.

Project Name and Number: The name of the project and number, if any, that has been assigned.

Purchase Order Number: The purchase order number as assigned by the people in the accounting department.

Purchase Order Allotment: The total amount (including services, expenses, etc.) allotted to the purchase order.

Invoice/Expense Report Date: The date that the vendor has typed in on his or her invoice or expense report.

Invoice/Expense Report Number: The invoice or expense report number that the vendor has typed on his or her invoice or expense report. These may include numbers, letters, or some other numbering system established by the vendor.

✓: When the vendor actually receives payment for the invoice, place a check mark beside the invoice or expense number.

Payment To: The name of the vendor who has sent the invoice.

Payment For: The purpose for which the invoice has been approved. This may be the project milestone (Start Up, Completion of Drafts, Completion of Masters, etc.) or simply a project expense (shipping, catering, etc.).

Amount of Payment: The dollar amount of the payment requested by the vendor on the invoice or expense report.

Cumulative Payments: A running total of all invoices and expenses as they are approved for payment.

Amount Remaining: The total remaining on the purchase order after cumulative payments have been deducted.
(Purchase Order Allotment - Cumulative Payments = Amount Remaining)

Project Name and Number: New Product Training, NP1234

Purchase Order Number: 000111   **Purchase Order Allotment:** $50,000

Invoice/Expense Report		✓	Payment To	Payment For	Amount of Payment	Cumulative Payments	Amount Remaining
Date	**Number**						
5/1	AB231	✓	ABC Design	Start Up	$10,000.00	~~$10,000.00~~	~~$40,000.00~~
5/20	751-XYZ	✓	XYZ Catering	Lunch, Focus Group	75.00	~~10,075.00~~	~~39,925.00~~
7/10	AB232		ABC Design	Blueprint	10,000.00	20,075.00	29,925.00

↑ As each invoice from a vendor is received, add its payment amount to this column and then cross out the previous total.

↑ This is the amount of the "Purchase Order Allotment" that is remaining after each invoice is deducted. Update the total as each new invoice is received.

NOTE: The total "Amount Remaining" and "Cumulative Payments" should add up to the "Purchase Order Allotment."

INVOICE TRACKER

Project Name and Number:_____

Purchase Order Number:_____ **Purchase Order Allotment:**_____

Invoice/Expense Report		✓	Payment To	Payment For	Amount of Payment	Cumulative Payments	Amount Remaining
Date	Number						

Conclusion

Vendors can make a powerful contribution to your instructional development projects. They can also use up enormous amounts of money and require extra time to manage and coordinate their efforts. However, if you select them carefully and take a systematic approach in directing their efforts, they can help you attain excellent results, on time and within your budget. The guidelines and methods described in this appendix will help you work more effectively with vendors.

Appendix B:

Manager Activities Summaries

As the first chapter pointed out, to be a successful project manager you don't need to be directly involved in all the events that take place during a project. However, beginning with Step 4: Develop the Blueprint, you must carefully plan each event, provide the stimulus to get the event started, and then intervene when needed to keep things running smoothly. Figure 1 illustrates this process.

This appendix is a summary of the recommended manager activities from Step 4 through Step 10 of the project management model.

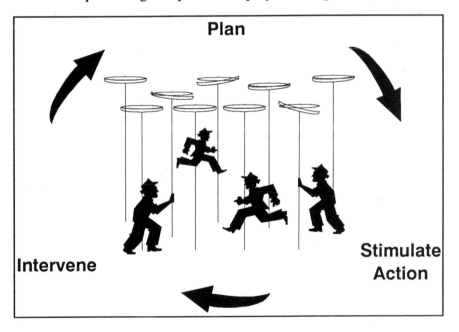

Figure B-1: Main Activities of a Project Manager

Activity \ Manager Role	Plan	Stimulate Action	Intervene
Brainstorm	Review budget and schedule Review alternatives	Discuss instructional alternatives	Reduce alternatives to a realistic few
Develop the Blueprint	Find or make examples of blueprint	Share examples with designers; Set deadlines	Examine samples of each ID's blueprint
Quality-Assure	Assemble QA criteria	Get blueprint from each ID and QA	Provide feedback
Distribute to Reviewers	Prepare sponsor and SMEs	Send blueprint and provide guidelines for review	Call and check progress
Obtain Feedback and Signoff	Set up meeting for feedback	Start meeting; Review blueprint page by page	Keep team focused; Obtain signoff

Manager Activities: **DEVELOP THE BLUEPRINT**

Activity \ Manager Role	Plan	Stimulate Action	Intervene
Create Draft Materials	Find or make examples of drafts	Share examples with designers; Set deadlines	Examine samples of each ID's drafts
Quality-Assure	Assemble QA criteria	Get drafts from each ID and QA	Provide feedback
Distribute to Reviewers	Prepare sponsor and SMEs	Send drafts and provide guidelines for review	Call and check progress
Obtain Feedback and Signoff	Set up meeting for feedback	Start meeting; Review drafts page-by-page	Keep team focused; Obtain signoff
Revise for Testing	Obtain annotated copy of drafts	Set deadlines for revision	Compare revisions to annotations

Manager Activities: **CREATE DRAFT MATERIALS**

Activity ↓ / Manager Role →	Plan	Stimulate Action	Intervene
Obtain Test Subjects	Review audience assumptions; List requirements	Contact sponsor; Request attendees; Set deadlines	"Nag" as needed
Prepare for Test	Determine evaluation strategy; Review logistics	Assign responsibilities; Set deadlines	Check progress
Conduct Test	Prepare and review ground rules	Start session; Coordinate observers	Keep test moving; Check obervers' notes
Debrief	Review debriefing strategy	Conduct debriefing sessions	Keep discussions focused and relevant
Determine Revisions	Analyze data gathered	Meet with IDs and sponsor; Specify revisions	Negotiate; Obtain signoff

Manager Activities: **TEST DRAFT MATERIALS**

Activity ↓ / Manager Role →	Plan	Stimulate Action	Intervene
Orient Producers	Prepare overview; Assemble latest drafts	Meet with producers; Show how pieces fit together	"Sell" design strategy; Discuss producer concerns
Establish Production Method/Schedule	List requirements of production design and schedule	Agree on production design/schedule with producers	Defend instructional integrity and sponsor's deadlines
Review Samples	Set deadlines for getting samples of each medium	Review and approve samples; Involve sponsors	Note deviations from the design; Specify revisions
Attend Production Sessions	Assemble and review draft materials and scripts	Attend production; Compare planned to actual	Note deviations from plan; Specify revisions
Obtain Sponsor Approval	Set up meeting to review masters; Assemble masters	Review masters with sponsor; Specify revisions	Keep sponsor focused; Get signoff

Manager Activities: **PRODUCE MASTER MATERIALS**

Manager Role → / Activity ↓	Plan	Stimulate Action	Intervene
Orient Repro./Dist. Team	Prepare overview; Assemble approved masters	Meet with producers; Show how pieces fit together	"Sell" design strategy; Discuss team concerns
Confirm Repro./Dist. Method/Schedule	List requirements of repro./dist. method/schedule	Agree on methods and schedule with team	Defend sponsor requirements; Discuss concerns
Review Samples	Set deadlines for getting samples of each medium	Review and approve samples; Involve sponsors	Note deviations from the design; Specify revisions
Inspect Storage & Distribution System	Assemble specifications; Set up inspections	Visit storage, distribution sites; Inspect	Note deviations from plan; Specify changes
Obtain Sponsor Approval	Plan review of sample copies and distribution method	Review samples and distribution method with sponsor	Note required changes; Get signoff

Manager Activities: **REPRODUCE & DISTRIBUTE**

Manager Role → / Activity ↓	Plan	Stimulate Action	Intervene
Define Objectives & Strategy	Discuss with sponsor, consumers of training	Meet with team; Determine objectives & strategy	Keep team focused on key issues
Develop Tools	Set deadlines; Provide samples	Review and approve tools; Involve sponsor	Note deviations from strategy; Specify changes
Implement Strategy	Schedule observations, interviews, etc.	Observe evaluation team in action	Note deviations from strategy; Get back on track
Synthesize & Analyze	Set deadlines; Remind team of key objectives	Meet with team; Review patterns, supporting data	Keep team focused on evaluation objectives
Report & Recommend	Provide team with report outline; Confirm deadlines	Review and approve draft report; Present to sponsor	Discuss sponsor concerns; Clarify and revise

Manager Activities: **EVALUATE**

ID Project Management

Suggested Readings and References

Beer, V. and Bloomer, A., Levels of Evaluation. *Educational Evaluation and Policy Analysis, 8*(4), Winter 1986, 335-345.

Bergman, R. and Moore, T., *Managing Interactive Video/Multimedia Projects.* Englewood Cliffs, NJ: Educational Technology Publications, 1990.

Bowsher, J., *Educating America: Lessons Learned in the Nation's Corporations.* New York: John Wiley, 1989.

Briggs, L., Gustafson, K., and Tillman, M. (Eds.), *Instructional Design: Principles and Applications.* Englewood Cliffs, NJ: Educational Technology Publications, 1991.

Brooks, F., *The Mythical Man-Month: Essays on Software Engineering.* Reading, MA: Addison-Wesley, 1982.

Davies, I., *Competency Based Learning: Technology, Management, and Design.* New York: McGraw-Hill, 1973.

Davies, I., *Instructional Technique.* New York: McGraw-Hill, 1981.

Diamond, R., *Designing and Improving Courses and Curricula in Higher Education.* San Francisco: Jossey-Bass, 1989.

Gagné, R., Briggs, L., and Wager, W., *Principles of Instructional Design.* New York: Holt, Rinehart and Winston, 1988.

Greer, M., Project Management: The Series. *Performance and Instruction Journal,* April 1988 - May/June 1989.

Gustafson, K., *Survey of Instructional Development Models.* Syracuse: ERIC Clearinghouse on Information Resources, Syracuse University, 1981.

Gustafson, K. and Reeves, T., IDioM: A Platform for a Course Development Expert System, *Educational Technology,* 30(3), March 1990, 26-31.

McCormack, M., *What They Don't Teach You at Harvard Business School: Notes from a Street-Smart Executive.* New York: Bantam, 1986.

Naisbitt, J. and Aburdene, P., *Re-inventing the Corporation.* New York: Warner Books, 1985.

Peters, T., *Thriving on Chaos: Handbook for a Management Revolution.* New York: Harper & Row, 1988.

Peters, T. and Waterman, R., *In Search of Excellence: Lessons from America's Best-Run Companies.* New York: Harper & Row, 1982.

Rossett, A., *Training Needs Assessment.* Englewood Cliffs, NJ: Educational Technology Publications, 1987.

Zemke, R. and Kramlinger, T., *Figuring Things Out: A Trainer's Guide to Needs and Task Analysis.* Reading, MA: Addison-Wesley, 1982.

Index

A

Audio-visual materials
  estimating materials required, 21
  production checkpoints for, 157
  production evaluation checklist
    for, 161-162
  reproduction evaluation checklist
    for, 173-174

B

Bidder's conference, 198, 205-207
Blueprint components, 109-110
Blueprint development, 110-118
  brainstorming instructional
    strategies, 112-113
  establishing consistent formats,
    113
  estimating materials required, 22
  estimating time needed, 35
  obtaining feedback and sign-off,
    117-118
  process summarized, 112
  project manager's role in,
    111-117, 220
  quality assurance, 114-116
  reasons for, 110-111
Brainstorming instructional
  strategies, 112-113

C

Consulting time, 26
Cost estimation, 45-62
  case study illustrating, 55-61
  labor costs, 45
  outside purchases, 45
  worksheet for, 46-54
Creating draft materials, 120-129
  establishing consistent formats,
    122-123
  estimating time needed for, 36
  obtaining feedback and sign-off,
    128
  process summarized, 123
  project manager's role in,
    122-129, 220
  quality assurance for, 123-127
  reasons for, 120
  revising for testing, 129

D

Designers, 70
  choosing carefully, 74
  information gathering
    responsibilities of, 105
  needs of, 92
Development time, 26-27
Distribution. *See* Reproduction
  and distribution
Draft materials
  See also Creating draft
    materials; Testing draft
    materials
  characteristics of, 120, 131
  described, 119-120
  quality assurance for, 123-127
  what to include, 121

E

Evaluation
  See also Follow-up evaluation
  estimating time needed for, 38
  levels of, 180-181
  manager's activities summarized,
    222
  production evaluation checklists,
    160-162

F

Feedback and sign-off
  for blueprint development,
117-118
  for draft materials, 128-129
Follow-up evaluation, 179-187
  assumptions of, 179
  defining objectives for, 183-184
  expert advice needed for, 180
  implementing strategy, 185
  levels of evaluation, 180-181
  process summarized, 183
  reporting and recommending,
    186-187
  selecting strategy for, 183-184
  synthesizing and analyzing data,
    185-186
  tasks in, 181-183
  tools for, 184-185
Follow-up phase, 9-10, 12-13
  See also Follow-up evaluation;
    Reproduction and distribution

I

Independent consultants, 196
Information gathering, 98-108
  checklist for, 101-103
  designers' responsibility, 105
  estimating time needed for, 35
  intervention guidelines for,
    106-107
  planning for, 99-104
  purpose of, 98
  sources of information, 98
  strategy checklist for, 101-104
  techniques summarized, 99
  worksheets for, 100, 104
Instructional developers. *See*
  Designers
Instructional development phase,
  7-9, 11-12
  See also Blueprint development;
    Creating draft materials;

software to assist with, 63
Project status reports, 78, 81
Project team, 68-75
    clarifying roles and
        responsibilities for, 84-85
    combining roles in, 73
    designers, 70, 74
    getting commitment to specific
        dates, 86-89
    production coordinator, 71, 92
    project manager. *See* Project
        manager
    reproduction and distribution
        team, 168-169
    roles and decision-making in, 75
    sponsors, 69, 73, 90, 91
    subject matter experts, 70, 73,
        80, 84-85, 91
    trainer, 71
Purchase orders, 212-214

Q

Quality assurance
    for blueprints, 114-116
    for draft materials, 123-127

R

Reproduction and distribution,
    166-178
    confirming methods and schedule,
        169-170, 175
    estimating time needed for, 37
    importance of quality in, 167
    inspecting storage and
        distribution system, 176, 177
    obtaining sponsor approval, 178
    orienting team, 168-169, 171-172
    process summarized, 167
    project manager's role in,
        167-178, 222
    reviewing samples, 170, 173-174
Reproduction and distribution team,

orienting, 168-169, 171-172
Request for proposal (RFP), 197
    guidelines for creating, 203-204

S

Sign-off
    for blueprint development,
        117-118
    for draft materials, 128-129
Sign-off forms, 79, 81
Sponsors, 69, 73
    needs of, 90, 91
    role in creating content, 84-85
Storage and distribution system,
    inspecting, 176, 177
Subject matter experts, 70, 73, 80
    listed in project diary, 80
    needs of, 91
    role in creating content, 84-85

T

Testing draft materials, 131-148
    debriefing, 141
    debriefing guidelines, 145
    defined, 132
    determining revisions needed,
        146-147
    estimating time needed for, 36
    guidelines for, 135-136, 142-145
    obtaining test subjects, 134-136
    preparing for test, 137-140
    process summarized, 133
    project manager's role in,
        133-148, 221
    reasons for, 132
    revising for, 129
    test preparation chores checklist
        for, 138-140
Time estimation, 26-44
    for blueprint development, 35
    case study illustrating, 39-43
    consulting time, 26

for creating draft materials, 36
development time, 26-27
for evaluation, 38
for information gathering, 35
for master materials production,
    37
for project organization, 34
for reproduction and
    distribution, 37
rules of thumb for, 33-38
saving time with more designers,
    38
for testing draft materials, 36
tools for, 27-38
worksheet for, 28-32
Trainers, 71

V

Vendor
    adhocracy, 195
    bidder's conference for
        selecting, 198, 205-207
    creating request for proposal
        for, 197, 203-204
    decision aid for using, 199-202
    defined, 191-192
    independent consultants, 196
    large national vendors, 193-194
    large regional vendors, 194
    negotiating contract with, 198,
        211
    paperwork associated with,
        212-217
    purchase orders and invoice
        trackers for, 212-217
    selecting and managing, 197-211
    selecting the best, 198, 208-210
    services provided by, 196
    types of, 192-196
Vendor adhocracy, 195
Vendor contract, 198, 211